## PETER HARNESS

Peter was born in Beverley in 1976 and grew up on the coast of East Yorkshire before reading English at Oriel College, Oxford (where he was President of the Oxford Revue). Currently, he lives in South London. His other writing for the stage includes an adaptation of *The Picture of Dorian Gray* and several comedy shows. Screenplays include *The Chocolate Dillionaire* for Film Four; *Where the Humans Go to Die*; and *The Waters of Babylon*, a BBC 2 film which won a Dennis Potter Screenwriting Award.

## OWEN McCAFFERTY

Born in 1961, Owen lives with his wife and three children in Belfast. His work includes *Shoot the Crow* (Druid, Galway, 1997; Royal Exchange, Manchester, 2003); *Mojo Mickybo* (Kabosh, Belfast, 1998); *No Place Like Home* (Tinderbox, Belfast, 2001); *Closing Time* (National Theatre, London, 2002); and *Scenes from the Big Picture* (National Theatre, London, 2003). Most of his work has been published by Nick Hern Books.

## RONAN O'DONNELL

Ronan lives in Edinburgh. His work includes *The Chic Nerds* (Traverse Theatre, Edinburgh, 1998); *Spambam* (commissioned for LOOKout Theatre Company for a Scottish tour, 2002; also performed at the Melbourne Festival by Lightbox Theatre Company, 2003); an English/Scots translation of Aristophanes' *Lysistrata* (Common Force Community Theatre, 2003); a translation/version of Xiaoli Wang's *In the Bag* (Traverse Theatre's International Playwrights in Partnership scheme, 2003); and *The Doll Tower*, a play based on the life of T.E. Lawrence and his Scottish bodyguard John Bruce. Two other short plays, *Monster* and *Amy Rose*, have also been published.

# SINGULAR
# (male)
# VOICES

## MONGOOSE
Peter Harness

## COLD COMFORT
Owen McCafferty

## BRAZIL
Ronan O'Donnell

**NICK HERN BOOKS**
London
www.nickhernbooks.co.uk

**A Nick Hern Book**

*Singular (male) Voices* first published in Great Britain
as a paperback original in 2004 by Nick Hern Books Limited,
14 Larden Road, London W3 7ST

Typeset by Country Setting, Kingsdown, Kent CT14 8ES
Printed and bound in Great Britain by Cox and Wyman Limited,
Reading, Berks

A CIP catalogue record for this book is available from
the British Library

ISBN 1 85459 760 4

# Contents

**Publisher's Note**

Plays for single actors – monologues, if you like – are difficult
to publish. For one thing, they are very short on the page, self-
evidently having no gaps between the dialogue, with the result
that a book containing one play for one actor rarely looks
substantial enough to stand by itself. For another, selling a set
of scripts to the whole cast of the original or subsequent
productions is hardly a recipe for huge sales. And for yet
another, they usually lack that *x* factor that makes people want
to buy plays they've just seen on stage. Tricky to define the
*x* factor, but it's got something to do with leaving the audience
feeling that they've seen something interesting happening but
they haven't quite grasped all the implications at one sitting.
So they need to consult the text to find our what they might
have missed. Caryl Churchill has the *x* factor in spades. Tony
Kushner too. But it's quite unusual for one-character plays to
have it.

So when I sat down to read *Mongoose* and *Brazil*, two plays
which had been submitted independently of each other but that
I had not seen on stage, I was feeling pretty negative about the
chances of getting them into print. Having read them, though, I
found them difficult to dismiss. I started mulling over ways of
publishing these two remarkable plays without running foul of
the problems mentioned above. One way might be to put them
into a volume together. Though dissimilar in so many ways,
they did at least share a singularity of character (in both senses
of that word). And there is supposedly safety in numbers.

But two plays didn't seem enough to make a volume; whereas
three seemed just right. And when I was invited by Owen
McCafferty, whose work I had already published, to a rehearsed
reading of his new play, *Cold Comfort*, at the National Theatre
Studio, I realised that here was my third 'singular voice'.
(Unfortunately, an anticipated production at the Dublin Theatre
Festival hasn't – at the time of writing – happened, but there's

no way that a piece of writing like *Cold Comfort* can remain
unproduced for long.)

Viewing the volume as a whole, I realise it has an extraordinary,
if largely fortuitous, coherence, even though the three plays are
so different – not least in their authors, who represent that
pleasing symmetry: an Englishman, an Irishman and a Scotsman.
We encounter three refreshingly distinct and distinctive voices
each put to the service of a single male character, who, like the
Ancient Mariner, insists on buttonholing us with his own
disturbing story. Short stories of this quality would win prizes.

If this volume finds a readership – and if there are people who
want to perform the plays in it – I shall indulge the idea that's
already beginning to form: a volume of plays for a single
female actor. Suggestions are welcome . . .

Nick Hern
October 2004

MONGOOSE

Peter Harness

*For Ragna*

*Mongoose* was first presented by Azi Eftekhari at the Southwark Playhouse, London, on 14 April 2003, with the following cast:

TED                              Richard Bremmer

*Director*   Thea Sharrock
*Designer*   Rachel Blues
*Lighting Designer*   David Plater
*Sound Designer*   Carolyn Downing

*Stage Manager*   Rebecca Pownall
*Assistant Producer*   Hannah Bentley
*Production Manager*   Tom Wright

The production was funded by a TIF/SOLT New Producers' Bursary financed by the Society of London Theatres and supported by the Arts Council of England, the Mackintosh Foundation, Clear Channel Entertainment and the Equity Trust Fund.

The author would like to express his profound gratitude to those bodies mentioned above. He would also like to thank The Peggy Ramsay Foundation for their generosity, Richard Bremmer and Thea Sharrock for their help in honing the original script, and most especially, Azi Eftekhari for her kindness, selflessness and dedication.

**Character**

TED, *a late middle-aged farmer*

*A messy farmhouse living room: dirty and decrepit. The only
furniture of any importance is a stained old armchair, a
sideboard upon which sit a bottle of whisky, a glass, and a
broken clock, and inside of which are several dirty and
battered cardboard boxes, taped up. TED, a late middle-aged
farmer, stands amongst the clutter, looking out of a window
which is presumably contained within the fourth wall. Grim-
faced.*

TED *mutters to himself for several moments.*

TED. Well, that's how it is.

> *Mutters to himself again, gets up, walks slowly across the
> room. He pours himself a glass of whisky, thoughtful. Brings
> glass to the armchair, and sits. As he does so:*

It was just about getting to *that* time of night . . . couple of
hours after sunset and – well, I should say, four or so hours
before I could go to bed – and Dad was just helping himself to
another glass of whisky, when – there was this odd sort of
noise . . .

> *With his long fingernails, he scratches three times, carefully
> measured, on the arm of the chair.*

The old feller shoots me the usual sort of glance, as if to say
'now then', and goes back to concentrating on his booze.

But it wasn't me this time. No. And I rather wanted to get up
and see what it *was*, but . . . Well, in any case, twenty minutes
later it came again. Interrupted him this time. Just nicely
started wagging his finger, when – (*Scratches again.*) So, of
course he could tell that it was nothing at all to do with me. He
looked around for a minute, belched, remembered what he'd
been saying, forgot about the noises, and started off again,
wagging his finger. Dad wasn't the sort to get out of his chair
unless he'd been seriously provoked. And that being the case, it
wasn't for another half hour or so, when the scratches had

come again, and shut him up again, that I took him out into the hall, and we had ourselves a little listen.

. . . I always liked our hall. Nice and cool and quiet. You could stop there for breath. And that's where we did stop . . . Dad was breathing close to. Everything else was silent. And there was this funny feeling in my guts, like I was nervous . . . Then it came

*Scratches again, joining in with his voice this time.*

Scratch. Scratch. Scratch. I caught myself standing out there again this morning, in the dark. Doing the self-same thing: really *listening*.

*Pause.*

'So that's it, then,' the old feller decided, '*rats!*' He thought they were trapped inside the walls. Making nests. F-f-fuh-fuh-fuh-funny sound for rats, I thought. 'Bugger what you think,' said Dad, 'get down to Turner's tomorrow, buy a tin of arsenic.' . . . He was in love with bloody poison, I think. Poison coming out of his bloody *ears*, almost! Poison for ants, weeds, rats, so on. 'Now, everything's got a poison, Ted,' he used to say, 'it's a tool. Take advantage.' That's what he used to say. Of course, I've never liked it. I don't see the point. Kill something with a gun, can't you, if you want to? I know you can't necessarily kill an ant with a gun. Or a weed, but . . . You can *boil* 'em! Get 'em by the neck and yank 'em up, lob 'em on the compost heap . . . We couldn't find out where it was coming from. And it didn't come again that evening, so after another few hours of the usual, we went up to bed . . . And the rest of the night was fairly quiet. Except somewhere, sometime in the dead hours, the cat woke us up, yowling. Crying down there in the dark, fighting with something or other.

*Pause.*

I talk to myself a lot these days.

*Pause.*

Well. No one else left to do it.

*He thinks for a moment, gets up, and goes to the sideboard.*

*He takes out many boxes – almost more than the sideboard could reasonably hold – finds the one he wants, produces a pocket-knife, and slits open the box carefully.*

It had been a pretty stormy patch we'd been having that autumn, so I thought it was probably something to do with that. I mean – you get used to it, living on a farm. Rats come down from the fields, and they try to get out of the rain by infesting your premises. And they'd infested us, the little so-and-sos, if the noises were anything to go by. (*Confidentially.*) Which they weren't. They got worse, see. All sorts of funny rackets. Knocks in the walls. Scratches on the doors. Little feet, scampering over the floors in the attic. (*Wistfully.*) . . . Little feet.

We weren't used to noise then. And it *was* noisy. Dad was . . . well, he was set in his ways, but I didn't mind it. I was young. Open-minded. I listened to the radio. It gave us something to *do* of an evening: talking about the noises. Following them around. 'There it is,' Dad'd shout, 'There it is, behind the clock!' 'No, Dad, it's over b-buh-by the buh-buh-' 'Bollocks. It's behind the bloody clock!' Every night, tracking them, chasing 'em. All we thought about. It was all we *could* think about. Leaving little grains of arsenic here and there. Filled the place up with 'em almost. And all of them vanished. So we thought we'd see an end to it soon, my little bit of interest . . . But we didn't.

It had been a relatively quiet few days. Two, maybe three weeks into it by now. Still no info. And I was not long off the school bus one afternoon, just nicely got home, fetching him down a box of liver salts, when – this *thing* appears. Slap bang in front of my nose. Out of nowhere. And bugger me if it's not a little tin soldier. Red tunic, black helmet, blue pants. And it stays there, about five-and-a-half foot off the ground, hovering, couple of seconds or more, and then (*Slaps the box.*) bang! – drops to the floor.

*He begins rummaging in the box.*

I just – I just *pelted* out of there, you know. Fast as I could go . . . Funny now, I suppose, but *then* . . . (*Shudders.*) Uph! . . . Oddly enough, all I wanted was my dad. To make it better.

I wouldn't let him go. Made a real pest of myself. Of course,
he didn't know what to make of it – I mean, I'd not been so . . .
I'd not been clutching at him like that since . . . since I was a
little boy. I even huddled in close to him when the noises
started up later. Tried to get hold of his hand. 'What are you
doing?' he said. 'Piss off.' And gave me a clout.

*He produces a tin soldier from the box*

Here it is. Nice little feller. Found him again under my pillow
after I went to bed that night. And I was too upset to be scared
then.

*He sets the soldier carefully on the arm of the chair, smiles
at it.*

Stand at ease. Plenty more where you came from, aren't there?
'Yes, Sergeant Ted!'

*He begins rooting in the box again and produces a very
small stone statuette, dirty and chipped.*

There! What about her, then? Isn't she just – isn't she a peach!
A real peach. Little Egyptian goddess, or princess or summat, I
can't rightly remember. Known as Mrs Ali-Baba to me. Three
thousand years old, apparently . . . Well, three thousand and
forty-three, now.

*He sets her down next to the soldier.*

There you go, sit with Private Bang.

*He rummages in the box, takes out a small newspaper
parcel, and opens it.*

*Roman* coins, look!

*Takes out a couple – they could be anything – black and
dirty.*

Gold. They're not bronze. Need a bit of a clean, maybe.
Emperor Claudius or something. Yep. There's dozens of these
little presents. Scattered about. I have a couple in the
nightstand next to my bed. That was really the plus side of that
period. Trinkets. Whenever – . . . Whenever the old man and
myself weren't – well, how do we put it? – seeing eye to eye,

whenever I'd left something out or I hadn't done something I
was supposed to, or whenever they'd . . . you know . . . I'd find
a little present . . . Under my bed sheet, in my little den. Once
on the sink when I was peeling the parsnips. Yes. The best one
was my birthday. I was just fetching another bottle of whisky
out of the larder, when who should turn up but Porky Pig! Just
out of thin air! A little . . . a little bakelite toy. (*Confidentially.*)
I'll tell you where he came from. He came from Burkett's.
Been in their window. I'd wanted him. I even had a little
money box with a copper or two saved up. But – the little
bugger had nabbed him for me . . . Or maybe he hadn't, I don't
know. Maybe he conjured him up out of somewhere. That was
him being magical, you see. Him being nice . . . Which is the
side I like to remember.

> *He notices an old piece of newspaper sitting in the box,*
> *picks it up, scans it, his face gradually falling. With sudden*
> *violence, he crumples it with both hands, and drops it into*
> *the box.*

The rest is just newspaper clippings.

> *Suddenly, he bursts into loud, wholehearted song:*

Oh, what a *beauty*!
I've never seen one as big as that before! (Have a ba-*na*-na!)
Oh, what a *beauty*!
It must be two foot long or even more!
It's such a lovely colour, and nice and round and *fat*!
I – (*Giggles.*) I never thought a *marrow* could grow as big
    as that!

> *Long, uncontrollable giggle, gradually disappearing into*
> *miserable silence as he gets up, pours himself another drink*
> *and goes to look out of the window.*

Winter's not a good time. Not anywhere . . . Stuck inside.
Can't get out to work . . . Old folk go soft in the head for
similar reasons . . . Start sitting inside on your own, you bring
it all out again, and you make yourself *eat* it, don't you? . . .
'S what I used to get cross with him about, towards the end.
(*Indicating boxes.*) Used to ask me to take down all this *stuff*
from out of the sideboard. Wanting to look through it. 'Why?'

I used to say, '*Why*? You'll only end up all difficult. I'll only have you fidgeting on my shoulder all night, keeping me up . . . You're as bad as bloody Dad used to be.'

*Pause.*

Well. I suppose it made a bit of a change. Tea just nicely gone down. Fire lit through here. I'd have my glass of whisky, he'd have his pot of double cream.

*He takes his drink and returns to the chair. Sits.*

I don't know why I have to think about *him*. You do your bloody best, don't you? Not good enough for some folk. (*Sniffs.*) No.

*Pause. He looks over the boxes.*

Come on, Ted.

*Produces knife, slits a nearby box open.*

Now, 'GOBSHITE' is *not* the most auspicious word to start things off with. Not given some of the lovely ones we had in between. Words.

*He roots out an old exercise book. Flicks through.*

But 'GOBSHITE' it was. (*Reads.*) G-O-B-S-H-I-T-E. And quite why it had to go in my English book, I've no idea.

*He holds it up to the light.*

'Have *I* written that?' I thought to myself. And when *they* notice it, they say to themselves, 'Has *Ted* written that?' They got Dad into school on one occasion, I don't know why, talking to him. I could see 'em through the door. They'd told me to wait outside. He was shifting about, scratching his head. '*I* don't bloody understand,' he says, 'fourteen bloody years old, he hasn't even learned to *speak*.'

*Searches out an old piece of paper, and scans it with a smile.*

This is nicer. (*Reads.*) 'Friend' . . . That's what he was to me. Not 'GOBSHITE' . . . A noisy, magical little friend who gave me presents and *wrote* to me. Dinnertimes, me and Dad'd sit

across from each other, eating beans. Usual elongated silence.
Him looking at me, sideways, like he used to. But I'd be
thinking to myself, 'I kn-nuh-nuh-nuh-*know* something you
don't know!' (*Laughs.*) Yes!

*A longer laugh. Dives into box, brings out a sheaf of*
*assorted papers.*

There'd be a little note in my pocket, like this. (*He rustles the*
*paper happily.*) With all sorts of *secrets* on it. Usually one for
me first thing, usually one waiting when I came back from
school.

*He looks through notes, reads one, emphatically.*

'I am a troublesum *mongoose.*' (*Laughs.*) 'Some' spelt 's-u-m',
of course. (*Finds another, reads.*) 'The mongoose likes a bowl
of milk. Leave the bowl beside the front door, may it please
you, Ted.'

*He looks through the other letters.*

Never seemed sure whether to call himself 'the mongoose',
you know, or whether to call himself 'me'. (*Reads.*) 'I like
a good dance, and don't mind if you play the wireless once
in a while, Ted. Please buy raisins. They keeps my belly in
order.' . . . He did like a good dance. (*Sings:*)

No one to talk to,
All by myself,
No one to talk to,
'Cause I'm happy on the shelf.
Ain't misbehavin'
Saving my life for you . . .

One of his favourites, that one.

*He smiles sadly, and slices open another box, which is full*
*of decrepit Christmas decorations.*

Always made a big deal of Christmas. At least we tried to, him
and me. Winter's just winter without it, isn't it?

*He produces a battered Christmas-tree fairy from the box.*

. . . This is Mam's. Used to help her with the decorations the
night before, and there'd be a big warm fire, and I'd be in my

jim-jams. Then Dad used to come in, all cold – you could almost smell the cold on his coat, you know – dragging the tree along the passage, up the steps. Branches bending on the door. And he always had something in his pocket, when she were . . . when Mam was . . . A packet of sweets or something, or biscuits, that I could reach in and get my hands on. She'd make him a nice warm bath, then we'd dress up the tree, and she'd got her arms around me and lift me up, so I could pop this on top . . . The Christmas after she . . . I remember, he'd come in, tired-looking, and I'd reached in his pocket . . . but there wasn't anything there. A bit of wire and a screwdriver, that was it. 'There's nowt there, lad,' he said, 'not this year.'

Twenty-fourth of December *that* year, we were in here, my dad and myself. (*Gestures.*) That clock what's stopped coming up half past eight. No tree, although I'd hoped. He could have taken one down from the wood. He was talking into his booze. Chill getting in . . . And I was wondering whether Mongoose might start with his noises . . . We had a flashlight, see. A proper one. Used to use it when we followed the racket round. Part of the routine by then. And I think to myself, 'Well, Ted, shall we see if it needs a fresh battery?' And I'm fiddling with the end, trying to get inside the bugger, when . . . bloody Eagle Eyes cracks on, and gives me one of his looks. Raises his eyebrows. 'You're a bit bloody eager with that thing, aren't you?' he says, and there's a little smile, 'Do you know something I don't know?' 'Uh-uh-uh-uh-uh-uh-uh' – I couldn't get anything to come out. And in his book, I know, that's as good as a confession. I'd been a bit *too* interested. A bit too eager. So I took a good deep breath, waited for it . . . But instead he just looks at me a bit longer, and says, 'Go and get another bottle out, Ted, there's a good lad. Stop playing silly buggers.' So I walk off to the pantry. And it's all quiet.

The noises didn't come 'til later. Not 'til the dead time on Christmas morning. And it was – what-d-you-call-it? Pan-de-monium. Scratch, bang, clatter, bang, knock. And Dad's up out of bed. 'Is that *you*?' he's shouting. Bursts into my room. 'Is it? Is it? Is it bloody you?' 'Nuh-nuh-nuh-', and he comes in close, and turns on the light, and he *looks* at me. *Looks*: (*Imploring.*) '*Who is it, then*?' . . . There was a bit of a moment, then he tramps back out onto the landing. And I'm almost asleep again when he starts up *roaring* with laughter. 'I know who it is!' he's saying. 'I know who it is!' Laughs all over himself again. 'It's Father bloody Christmas!' . . . Well, if it was Father bloody Christmas, he did a bloody awful job.

*Pause.*

New Year's Eve came along . . . And . . . (*A little puzzled.*) We had some visitors . . . We never *used* to have visitors. Only the coalman and the bloke what brought the straw and such, but . . . well, this one New Year's Eve we did. Turned up, like visitors do, all big, and . . . full of noise, and . . . Dad says, 'You won't remember your Uncle Dennis and your Auntie Betty, will you?' He'd been shining his shoes. Of course I didn't bloody remember them. They were a pair of them make-believe uncles and aunties you get when you're little. Big beard, long red fingernails, that kind of – stuff.

So they come in, get 'emselves sat down. Laughter. Talking. And I don't know where to put myself. Wanted to stay upstairs. I wanted to get myself out of the way, have a look at the trinkets and so on . . . But they say, 'No, no, Ted, no, stay here. Keep us company.' And on they bloody go. He's going on – Dennis – about his ex, why and zed, and she's prattling about this and that, and Dad's . . . Dad was bloody well joining in. Talk, talk. And then they start – going on about Mam . . . Telling stories. She gets her handkerchief out, and Dad looks across at me and says, 'Go put the kettle on for Auntie Betty, will you?'

And I'd been in there about ten minutes. Because I didn't know what to do . . . Because . . . Because . . . when I'd come through the door . . . there it was . . . Smeared on the wall in . . . in . . . And he'd written, 'GET STUFFED AND BUGGER OFF, DENNIS AND BETTY'. And I was trying to attack it with a cloth, when she opens the door and comes in, wondering where her tea's got to.

*Pause.*

I got what I wanted. I got sent upstairs. Could still hear the sounds coming up through the floor. Talking. Two rumbles and a squeak. (*Sings*.) 'Old acquaintance be forgot.' And it's gone midnight and I've heard the front door go, and a car start up and drive away, when my bedroom door opens, bangs against the wall, and I feel the landing light on my face. I knew it was my dad, so I act like I'm asleep. Breathe deep. And you could hear him *thinking* for a while. Trying to work it all out. Then he comes forward and pulls me out of bed.

And after he's all finished I hear his feet scrape on the boards, door swing shut. And out beyond, regular sort of scratching in the wall, meaning Mongoose. Dad going after it, cracked-voiced, shouting . . . Then the noise of him falling backward down the stairs. Right the way to the bloody bottom.

*He gets up and shuffles to the door. Opens it, and looks into the hall. Pause. He shuts the door.*

They always used to ask me two questions . . . First one was, 'How did I *know* he was a mongoose?' Well . . . (*Thinks*.) He told me so . . . And he *looked* like a mongoose. You know. Fifty per cent weasel, fifty per cent cat. Pink extremities.

Sometimes, in later years, I just used to stretch my hand out around him. Feel his ribcage. Neck . . . And it'd hit me . . . Just how small and . . . unprotected he was. Ever such a little body. Warm. No bigger than a man's grip . . . I'd get him up close, and tuck his little blanket tight. Just to keep that little bit of warmth burning . . . Didn't work.

Didn't work . . . The other question was, '*Why* did it happen? Why did he come in the first place? Why to you?' Well . . . My answer's always been, 'Why does *anything* happen?'

*Pause.*

Little jaunt over Heatherlands Hill today, before it got too dark. Where him and me used to go and blow the cobwebs away, when he could manage it . . . Little sheep had died, poor thing. Frozen itself . . . If there's nowhere to get warm, and there's a snowdrift, they'll do that, you know. Bury themselves. Nice and snug to begin with, I should think. Silly buggers . . . I didn't have the stomach to skin it. Just packed it back in again and left it where it was . . . Well, such is life.

*Returns to the armchair.*

I was sitting in the waiting room at the cottage hospital,
looking through the *Eagle*, which to my mind was always full
of rubbish, when this tired-looking feller with a stethoscope,
and pubes in his ears, comes up alongside. 'Hello,' he says,
'how's tricks?' 'Not buh-buh-buh-buh,' I said. 'Glad to hear it,'
he says, ''cause your dad's in a bit of a mess.' Well, *I* could
have told him that, and I was just about to say something of
the sort, when I suddenly panic and think to myself, what if
he's using a what-d'you-m'call-it? Maybe Dad's duh-duh-
duh . . .

When Mam went, you know, they used all sorts of what-d'you-
m'call-its. Save my feelings. Auntie Vi comes in, imaginary
blackcurrants on her hat, and she says, 'You won't be seeing
Mam again, our Edward. She's gone to a better place,' and
gives me a tangerine . . . And I thought to myself, 'Well, she's
no business going to a better place . . . What's she doing going
off somewhere better and not taking me? I always go with her
to puh-puh-puh-puh-*Pickering*.'*

I just waited for her to get fed up of it and come back . . . But
I'm standing by the fence, one playtime . . . and Eileen
Bellamy comes up and says, 'Your mam's dead. My dad went
to 'er funeral.' I didn't know what to say . . . 'He's not duh-
duh-duh-duh,' I ask. 'No,' says the doctor, 'broke his legs', and
asks how old I am. And I was walking out past the flower beds,
when I suddenly thought, 'What would it be like if he *was*?'

And I went to Robinson's, and I bought a *pound* of Liquorice
Allsorts. And a *jar* of Blackjacks – a *jar*! And ten Player's, and
a bottle of cream soda!

*Pause. He gets up to look out of the window.*

Nobody thinks it's anything, these days, to be able to say what
the birds are called. But they should. (*Points.*) Jab your finger
out: 'That's a grebe.' 'That's a blackbird.' Worthless nowadays.

---

* If Ted is not played as a Yorkshireman – and there's no great need for him
to be – 'puh-puh-puh-puh-Pickering' can be substituted with the name of any
likely sounding town (beginning with a 'P', of course) that is local to his
accent.

No one gives a bugger. Not even about the names of the flowers.

But they should. If you didn't know what the birds are, you'd never know when the swallows were back, would you? If you didn't know what the flowers are, you wouldn't know what a snowdrop is. Then you'd be just like a baby. Helpless.

Animals as well. I've always been good at the identification of animals, ever since I was a little boy . . . He used to test me. Used to ask me, 'What am *I*, Ted?' And then I'd say, 'You are a mongoose.' 'Yes, Ted. A mongoose. Just so.'

Mam and me used to have this book. Full of everything. You know, wildlife matters. Pictures. Pictures were sometimes better than – . . . Names, as well. Spent hours with that little book. Took it rambling, down the lane. Up Heatherlands Hill . . . Two of us. Trying to find the little birds. Happy . . . You know.

*He purses his lips and tries to whistle.*

My lips have dried up . . . I could do all of 'em, once. The songs. Birds that wake you up in the morning just as the light's creeping in at the edge of the curtains. Chaffinches . . . (*Tries to whistle a chaffinch call, fails.*) Wrens . . . (*Tries to whistle a wren call, fails.*) Tits.

*He looks over the boxes.*

I'd drag it out, if I had it, that little book. But it's gone. Long since.

*Pause. He goes to sit down once more.*

It's a good long way to get here, you know. It's a trek. And there was just myself to do it. Sun had gone out of the sky, what'd kicked off the year. Bit uncertain now. Sweets had stuck themselves together in my pocket. Pop was gone flat. Fags'd turned my face green. I suppose, in a way, I'd got a bit vexed as I was walking up. Dad out of the picture. Nowt to defend myself with. Just me. Ready to turn my key.

So I got myself in, and I was in the kitchen, just making myself a bit of food, wanting to make it look proper, when I start off whistling a little birdsong to myself. Yellowhammer.

*Tries a yellowhammer call. Successfully.*

*Little-bit-of-bread-and-no-cheese.* When all of a sudden –
(*Another yellowhammer call.*) Out of nowhere. I suddenly got
that funny feeling again, like I had the night he first came. Put
down my dinner, stopped, listened. (*Another yellowhammer
call.*) 'Is that who I think it is?' I thought, or maybe I said it
out loud, 'Is that who I think it is?' And all of a sudden . . . the
room was filled with birdsong.

That was the *best* time, that little period. When Dad was in
hospital. We just got on . . . Me, working, fixing fences,
shepherding here and there. Him, busy with his affairs. He'd
write me a little note, first thing, when I'd done milking. Tell
me how pleased he was. And he'd do another when I was back,
at night. 'Let's have some sweets, Ted,' it'd be, 'Let's play the
wireless. Let's sing the birdsongs again, like that day in the
kitchen, Ted.' I'd even started catching sight of him. Tail
flicking off round a corner. Little feet scampering away. Hints,
you know. Suggestions. What it might be like, if he stuck
around, and we could just be left alone.

*Pause.*

I didn't *want* to go down there and see my dad . . . There he
was, stuck in his dirty plastercasts at the end of the ward. Same
face, same eyes. Same gob. 'If I find anything's been buggered
up, I'll *kill* you when they let me out.' Well . . .

Andy Paterson, he's our auctioneer, comes up next day, to take
off some of the cows. We're walking back from the top field,
and he asks if we'd still got them noisy rats. 'You'll have to get
some poison in,' he says, '*Christ Almighty*!' Bobs down. 'Is
this *your* cat?' . . . Yes, it was. Dead. 'It's sicked up all its . . .
Christ Almighty!' I look down at it and I say, 'Was all right
this muh-muh-muh-morning.' 'Well, it's dead now,' he says.
And there's a bit of questioning. 'There *is* only you, isn't
there?' he says. I was going to tell him, no, Andy Paterson,
there's that bloody mongoose. Only I thought better of it.
'Can't leave it spread out there, Ted. Flies'll lay eggs in that
gob.' . . . Well, it was the wrong time of year for flies.

Couple of days later, I found the dog, poisoned. Day or two
after that, the other dog we kept. Then it was open season.

Foxes – five or six of them, stretched out on a hay-bale in the barn. Badgers. Little family what'd set up home in Horseshoe Wood. Mam, Dad, Youngster . . . Then cattle. Every day, I'd open my eyes, and whisper to myself, '*Today*. Today, there'll be no grief, and there won't be nowt dead.'

*Pause.*

Never really understood that patch. His *reasons*, I mean. We were going through this stuff again, not so long since, and he'd dozed off and left me to it. And I was thinking . . . I mean, a reason for it maybe came to mind . . . See, I must've been pretty big to him then . . . I mean – like – *God*. To him . . . And I wondered, recently, if . . . if it was all some kind of sacrifice . . . And it gets to bothering me a bit. I mean, you don't like to think of folk sacrificing stuff to you, left, right and centre. So I woke him up, and, well, I came out with it. And he said that I was a fathead . . . And *then* he said – and I suppose this was a bit more thought through – that he'd never made a sacrifice for me that I didn't *need*. And nodded off. (*Sniffs.*) So I suppose that buggered that theory.

. . . *Or did it?, he wonders.*

You get a bit confused. Thinking things over.

I mean, he did his best to sugar it. Poisoning them creatures. Kept on with trinkets. Birdsong. Letters turning up like, 'I'd never kill a boy', or 'You and me'. *That* was when I got scared. I never told him this, not never, but I took to thinking, 'What's been unleashed? What's been let out? Can't we puh-puh-pack it all in again?' Hid in my room. Not talking. Not leaving him out his milk and nuts. But that just made him cross. Started then to find his voice, a bit. Could whisper bits and bobs. That was scary.

'Is that Ted?' Made me jump. Copper. 'You've shot up, haven't you?' The one from down the village. 'It *is* Ted, isn't it?' Well, he knew it was me. Just pissing about, he was. Who else would it be, standing up in the top field? 'What you up to?' he says . . . I was burying a cow. You could tell what he was thinking . . . What else could I do but bury it? I wouldn't have bloody ate it. There'd been a note, pinned on its arse: 'Do not eat this cow, Ted. I have poisoned it.' So I tip the thing in, and we wander off to the farm. Get him set with a cup of tea, and off he goes: ' "That old bitch your missus don't deserve nothing",' he says. " 'Not even a fatheaded gnome like yourself. Pybus the massive butcher puts meat in her gob he wouldn't sell at his shop. Yours faithfully, Ted, Langtoft Farm." Did you write this?' Pushes it across the table . . . Well, there wouldn't have been much use saying I didn't. Mongoose had done it in *my* handwriting.

'You can't do this, lad,' he says, 'Imagine how Mr Turmody felt, opening up *that.* Can you?' 'Nuh-nuh-no.' 'Like a proper twat, I would have thought.' There's a silence. 'That's three letters come from Langtoft now, Ted, to various folk. If there's a fourth, I shall have to put you on a charge. Understand?' I said nowt. And then he reaches over, and smacks me in the gob. 'Do-you-*understand*?'

And as I watched him pedalling off down the lane, I thought to myself, yes, I do. Understand. That's what you get for breaking friends.

> *He produces the knife, gets up, and walks through the boxes. Finds the one he wants, cuts it open, rummages, and pulls out a very small pink blanket. Pulls it close to him, strokes it, and sits down again. Keeps it in his hands, still stroking it.*

I do miss him. That little feller. Part of me. I know it sounds daft . . . He'd wake up when I came in, 'fore I got tea on the go, and we'd talk for a bit, just together. (*Gestures.*) He'd sit there. Go off into a doze.

I think that's what interested folk about him. That he was a talker. Could talk for hours. Not then. Not at the start . . . Not at the end, neither, poor old bugger. After a bit, though, after all (*Gestures to boxes.*) *this* . . . talk and talk and talk . . . Not about himself. Not selfish. Just listen right hard to what you had to say, for hours, sometimes. Never butt in. *Real* listening . . . Folk have a problem doing that. Too het up with what they want to say. Itching for you to shut your gob, so they can get their twopen'orth in . . . He wasn't like that. He wanted to know what *I* thought. He wanted to make me feel better. He wasn't *like* that . . . going about, poisoning stuff . . .

*Pause.*

I suppose it was maybe a *part* of him.

But he wasn't *like* that.

*Pause.*

Dad came back the next day. Been a message scrawled on the wall of his bedroom: 'This is the den. Please to remember what I did with the foxes.'

I got him upstairs, into bed, with a lot of pushing and shoving. Couldn't walk yet. Plenty of rest. 'What's this?' he's saying as we go up, 'What've you done there? Why haven't you done such-and-such?' He wasn't so bloody big any more. Difficult nursing anybody, I suppose. But worse if it's someone like my dad. He was on my back every hour of every bloody day. Needling me. Banging with his stick.

*Hammers against the arm of the chair, imitating his father.*

'Get me this, fetch me that, lift me on my potty, cook me my breakfast, milk the cows, feed me wash me get the shopping! Bang! BANG! *BANG!*' Christ, it was no bloody wonder!

There was a new routine after Dad came back. Nice, effective little pattern. Mongoose waited 'til after we were tucked up. Then started with the noises . . . I could sleep through it. I was tired. But Dad'd be awake and bolt upright so bloody fast you'd think his water bottle'd popped on him. Then everything'd go quiet. No knocking, no scratches. (*Laughs.*) And he'd sit there with all his hair all over the place, and his eyes bulging out, flailing about for his stick, *looking* for it, like Mother bloody Goose. And after a while, he'd lay back down, shaking his head, mumbling to himself, having another pill. And just when he was just nicely off to sleep again –

*He beats his fists against the arms of the chair.*

'What is it? What is it? What is it?' . . . Just a game, really. Asleep and awake. Asleep and awake. Every time he shut his piggy little eyes . . . You haven't to laugh, though, have you? Took its toll on him, the poor old sod.

But what could he do? Couldn't blame *me*. I was asleep.

*Pause.*

Don't sleep too well nowadays. Age.

*Pause.*

I'd opened a tin of sago, and took it up to him to eat. And as I go in to set it next to the bed, he grabs hold of me. 'Come here. *Come here.*' . . . Gets me down there next to him. 'I know what your game is, lad. *Keep still!*' And he tells me what he reckons I'm up to. Knocking at night. Hiding his painkillers. 'I can't get *any* bloody sleep. *Listen!*' 'Huh-hah-have your sago,' I say. 'Huh-*have* it.' He lets go, and whacks the bowl off across the floor. Smashes. White muck on the boards. 'I'll *kill* you when I get up,' he says. And all of a sudden, I'd had enough. I pull back, and can feel it coming in my neck, and my throat starts to hurt, and suddenly, it's there in my mouth, and I yell at him (*With terrific venom.*) '*You'll have to fucking get up first!*' And I ran out. Down the lane, up Heatherlands Hill.

*Gets up. Pours himself a drink.*

I'd already started talking to him again, started leaving him his milk. I needed him. I needed a friend. He'd took to sleeping in my closet. I could hear him breathing late at night.

*Pause.*

'I'm not going to hurt you, lad. You've just got to learn.' Been out for a while, thinking things over. Called in with another bowl of sago. 'Wh-wh-wh-what?' I asked. *What* did I have to learn? 'Your fuckin' bloody lesson.' And he smiles . . . I never once saw him smile because he was happy. Smiles meant something else . . . 'Wh-wh-wh-wh-what've you done?' And that smile just sits there on the edge of his mouth, hanging off of his lips. He could walk when he really wanted . . . Because while I was out, he'd hobbled off into my bedroom, and broken *everything*. All the special little things that mean a lot to little boys. Everything I had of Mam. He'd tore up our little wildlife book, and the little photograph I had of her and me . . . Old

clothes, old faces, holding hands like we did. And Blackpool
beach in the background, going on for ever.

*Pause.*

Mongoose got into bed with me later on that night. Snuggled
up. And I – *touched him*. For the first time . . . Warm. Soft.
Alive. He licked me with his rough little tongue.

And there it was in the morning, on my wall, written in Mum's
old lipstick, 'We'll fix the dirty bastard!' I didn't think to rub it
off. It came up in court.

They asked, 'Did it not strike you as odd, that your father
suddenly developed these *symptoms*?' . . . Well, I didn't think
about it. 'It's these bloody pills,' he'd said . . . Diarrhoea, you
know. Stomach pains. His hair dropped off. And he had this
funny little walk he developed. (*Stands.*) He'd get out of bed to
go and vomit, and he'd be –

*He does a strange little shuffle across the room, standing on
tiptoe. A mixture of the Count in* Nosferatu, *and Richard III.*

Comical.

*Stops, smiles, and sits down.*

'Why didn't you fetch the doctor?' they said.

*Pause.*

Well. That's the sixty-four thousand dollar question. Isn't it?

*Pause.*

The truth is . . . The more Dad got weak, the more Mongoose
got strong. Breaking things. Making noise. You couldn't have
brought anyone in. They wouldn't have understood. They'd've
added up the letters to Mr Turmody and co., the messages,
poisoned cat, little tin of arsenic, and come to the wrong
conclusion. That's what they would've done . . . Easy enough.
Only me to go on, otherwise . . . So no one came.

*Pause.*

The old man only ever cried once. And it wasn't like when he
smiled. You knew what it meant. Four or five days before he –

Mongoose had stuck a ruler in his mouth. Sideways. Gone in
during the night. Dad woke up, and his gums were dripping
blood, and his tongue was all swelled up, and . . . I had to cut
the side of his mouth to slip it out . . . I think that was his limit
reached. That was when he cried. Vomited. Crapped himself.
Talked, muttered. Just bits of rubbish you couldn't hardly hear,
or understand . . . And the night he . . . (*Vague smile.*) The
night he went to a better place . . . Mongoose danced. Happy.
Found his voice at last. Singing a dirty song.

*Starts to sing, very very slowly, deadpan:*

Oh, what a beauty!
I've never seen one as big as that before!
(Have a ba-na-na!)

*Silence.*

Prison, for a bit.

*Silence.*

But I don't think that's especially relevant . . . Then back up
here.

You couldn't hardly live up here, then. Full of dirt and dust.
Filthy. Been left here for years, some things. Gone rotten . . .
But I had to come back. *We* had to come back. Maybe it *did*
mean starting over, but . . . my *life* was in here, stuck amongst
the mess. Bits of Dad, of course, mainly . . . But there were
still some bits of Mam. And bits of Mongoose . . . I couldn't
have let it go. Left it. There'd be nothing whatsoever then . . .
Yes.

We got to work, fixing things up, got it liveable, just about.
Eventually . . . There'd be a deal of encouragement from him,
but . . . I had most of it to do myself. *He* couldn't fix things.
Couldn't clean things up like me. Only give advice. Could only
keep me going.

His mind was much clearer than mine, to tell you the truth.
Even if he was just a little animal. Thought much more about
the world than me. How it works. How folk are. Music,
history. Books. If it were Christmas . . . he'd maybe ask for a
little book on so-and-so, and over the winter, I'd read it to him.

As many words as I could manage. After dinner, when we got in here . . . Always wanted me to think, he did . . . And I didn't *mind* thinking, but . . . I'd rather just've had him *here*. Now.

*He gets to his feet, crosses to the sideboard, opens a drawer, and brings out a roll of parcel tape. He marshals the boxes, taping up the ones he has opened. He then methodically sets about lifting them up, and tucking them back in the sideboard. This takes some time, and as he does it, he continues speaking.*

I didn't want *events*. I'd *had* all the events. Winter going to spring's all right, spring to summer, autumn. That's all the events *I* want. Going through the year, ending where you started. That's enough . . . Winter'd mean a fire in here, I'd light in the morning, pop back every now and then to feed. Blaze on Christmas day. To keep him warm.

Only . . . the last few years, seemed just to make him sleepy. Used to curl up in the blanket, little thing, and sleep. And sleep . . . Lively enough in the summer, scampering about, wanting a journey up the hill. A lot of talk, a lot of new ideas. But winter . . . didn't have the will to get up to anything . . . Just going over old things again, we'd be . . . Yes.

*Pause.*

I didn't know that he'd died, when he did . . . 'Course, he was looking a bit old. But that comes to all of us. Don't mean we're any different. Different to what we were. We don't change, in my opinion. Just get stuff given us. Or took away . . . I thought it'd be the same for ever. Sitting in the same chairs, doing the same things. Keeping each other close. Together.

But one night . . . he'd asked me to get all this stuff out again, so we could look through it. *Again.* And I'd just nicely got it all laid out, so we could go through it after dinner, and I turned round, and . . . he'd just gone. Quietly gone.

*Pause. Everything is tidied away.*

Silly old mongoose.

*Pause.*

Just me now . . . To fix things up . . . Clear away the mess.

*Pause.*

You can't expect things to carry on for ever, can you?

*Pause.*

Well, that's how it is.

*Lights fade.*

# COLD COMFORT

## Owen McCafferty

**Character**

KEVIN TONER, *late thirties to early forties. Haggard, drunk.*

*The stage is empty but for three simple wooden chairs and a coffin. The coffin is resting on two similar chairs. Above is a bare light bulb. KEVIN is wearing an overcoat and suit but does not look neat. He carries a bottle of whisky. Removing the overcoat, he lets it fall to the ground. He inspects the suit – 'suit / fuck'. He pulls a chair close to the coffin and sits down. His actions are slow. He unscrews the bottle, looks at it, presents it to the coffin then takes a drink. He doesn't like the taste.*

words / talkin

*KEVIN stands over the coffin and takes a drink.*

never drink this shit y'know / only doin it cause a you like / muckers / give it a burl / i'm a vodka man me / better for ye / keeps the head clear / head must be clear / vodka's healthy / aye / sit

*Sits down and sets the bottle on the floor in front of him. 'Stay'. Pulls chair closer to coffin.*

drink's all bollocks anyway

*Settles himself.*

thought we might / we might have a yarn / just sit an have a yarn / talk / whatever / when we're over we're over / put the lid dixie on / that's it / y'know / that's the plan anyway

*Stands over the coffin displaying the suit.*

what ya reckon / can't see / no glasses on ye / put the glasses on

*Takes a pair of glasses from his pocket and puts them on the dead body.*

there ya go / see better now

*Displays the suit again.*

reckon it    /    better on me than you    /    suit

*Points to overcoat on the floor.*

and coat

*He sits down.*

me own clothes were a wee bit manky    /    big event y'know
/    didn't want people    /    where    /    didn't want people    /
tuckers    /    didn't want them thinkin i was a tosspot y'know    /
tosspot    /    it's better nobody's here anyway    /    gives us
time    /    people here you'd only have to talk to them    /    ya
wouldn't want that talkin to other people message would ye    /
not yer form    /    wee woman next door    /    different matter    /
you should thank the wee woman next door    /    she    /
lovely wee woman    /    sorted all this out    /    arrangements    /
salt of the earth wee woman    /    only for her be a bin bag job
up the entry    /    could happen all right    /    no matter    /
salt of the earth    /    give me readies for the gargle y'know    /
she knew the score    /    seen it all before    /    know by the
face    /    a put it on a wee bit like just in case    /    desperate    /
really desperate    /    all that trick    /    a put on for the readies
/    needed a gargle    /    both of us    /    needed a gargle    /
it's understood    /    lovely wee woman    /    brought her into
the other room an    /    offered her a gargle an that    /    do
things the right way    /    isn't that right    /    that's right    /
nobody fuckin here but still has to be done the right way    /
didn't want one    /    not the point    /    done right    /    lovely
wee woman    /    not gonna weigh in for the funeral like    /
apologised    /    doesn't go to them    /    doesn't like them    /
says the make her all sad    /    doesn't like bein sad    /    fuck    /
doesn't hold the copyrights for that does she    /    she yer girl    /
you an her in the big picture    /    that been yer lot has it    /
the wee woman next door    /    in the big picture with the wee
woman next door    /    no    /    didn't think so    /    lovely wee
woman

*Looks into the coffin.*

too good lookin for you wee man    /    ya don't look well    /
older    /    smaller    /    pokey wee face    /    the look of death
hasn't helped ye    /    works for some people    /    hasn't done
you any favours

*Takes a drink.*

know how i found out about all a this    /    i'm standin in this
pub    /    good day few shillins    /    kilburn    /    you wouldn't
know that    /    should know it but wouldn't    /    no    /    fuck
it ya know it now    /    standin in this boozer in kilburn    /
drinkin in the corner y'know    /    in the corner    /    don't want
to get involved    /    lookin but don't want to get involved    /
on ma jacks    /    havin a pint    /    too early for a biff    /
you'll understand this    /    pacin    /    everythin has to do with
pacin    /    that's me for the day    /    enough readies on me to
stand there an work away    /    has to be planned out    /    a
good day ahead    /    good days arc planned out    /    get
yourself full    /    than the evening shift weighs in    /    that's
another story    /    if you're lucky    /    next thing this guy's
standin face to face with me    /    kevin toner isn't it    /    aye    /
it's me micky walsh    /    know this guy from away back    /
from here like    /    met him on sites now an again    /    drinker
/    drank with him    /    i was thinkin that's the plan finished    /
haven't seen this guy in years    /    he's fuck all to do    /    i
pop into his napper an he takes a chance    /    on the tap    /
no way he's readies on him an he's coming round to buy me a
gargle    /    on the tap    /    that's the way my head's thinkin    /
stick it out    /    do a runner    /    or tell him to fuck off    /
some geezer a hardly knew goin mess my day up    /    wha    /
y'know what it's like yourself    /    settled in    /    comfy    /
there's expectations about the way things are goin to go    /
days like this only once in a while    /    can't have that fucked
about    /    no point in doin a runner his head's fixed on the
gargle    /    he'd find me    /    can't stick it out cause a don't
want to be sippin a pint half the fuckin day    /    tellin him to
fuck off could end up in nasty pills    /    either buy him a
gargle or pretend a don't know him    /    pretendin a don't
know him will work    /    ya just keep sayin it until the leave    /
the problem with this guy is he'll know it's a spoof so he'll
hang in there an try an wear me down    /    fuck it    /    what
do ya want micky a pint    /    i'll get you one he says    /
happy fuckin days    /    he's on a bender must have a tank    /
order a biff    /    bad news he says    /    what bad news    /
haven't seen him in a fuckin lifetime    /    know big liam    /
foreman we used to    /    aye    /    dead    /    no not him    /

his mate patsy worked on the roads  /  aye dead  /  no not
him  /  he has a sister  /  she dead  /  no not her  /
she's married to roger the painter  /  don't know him  /  ya
must do he says  /  he says that's as far back as he knew
anyway so it didn't matter  /  somebody was back here who
met somebody who knew me or whatever  /  bad news  /
yer da's dead  /  in like flynn make that a double i said  /
micky's forkin out  /  i was about to buy not me kid i don't
have a da  /  then a remembered a did  /  been a while
y'know  /  forgot about ye  /  two of us pissed  /  then
next thing i'm on a plane  /  micky forked out again  /
said somethin about yer da only dyin once  /  one way ticket
like  /  here a am  /  smoke fuckin signals  /  didn't know
why or how or anythin  /  wee woman next door she said  /
lyin for four days  /  stone cold  /  this suit maybe  /
lyin there  /  that's why ya look ill  /  make ya sick  /
no fucker to  /  to help ya  /  i'm here now an a don't want
no more talk about it  /  right  /  no thankin me  /  scrub
that  /  at the same time  /  don't be fuckin  /  don't be
gettin all fuckin high on yer horse here  /  that's not  /
that's not what's happenin  /  not on  /  just leave it  /
just say fuck all  /  i say fuck all  /  you say fuck all  /
understood  /  bright man that ya are  /  fuck all  /  right
/  just here

*He takes a drink, then puts the top back on the bottle. He
takes the top back off the bottle has another drink then
throws the top away.*

etiquette  /  a mean  /  what i expected to be doin  /
understand i'm gonna  /  gonna get full  /  would've been
gettin full anyway  /  regardless of yer circumstances  /
look  /  haven't see each other for a while so  /  so i'll tell
you about me  /  you tell me about you  /  simple  /
keep it simple stupid  /  that all right doin that  /  pass the
time  /  before we know it it'll all be over  /  screw the
chats down  /  alright  /  here we go  /  i live in kilburn  /
drinker  /  an a live in a flat on ma tod  /  right you go  /
you live in belfast  /  yer a drinker  /  an you live in a
house on yer tod  /  i was married an now i'm not  /  you
were married now you're not  /  we're like fuckin twins  /

two peas in a pod   /   spat each other out   /   fuckin twins   /
tell me why'd ya never talk   /   why'd ya never fuckin talk   /
silent fuckin business   /   treatment   /   thoughts   /   runnin
around there inside your napper   /   just weavin their fuckin
way round inside yer head   /   not lettin them out   /
thoughts about your thoughts   /   wha   /   (never lettin them
out)   /   i used to be sittin there with ma ma   /   know when
a was a kid   /   i could never understand this y'know   /
never could   /   you'd come in an sat down in yer chair   /
same message every night   /   she'd be ragin   /   absolutely
fuckin ragin   /   bangin shit about an that   /   hard face on
her   /   i could never understand what that was about   /
there was never a word out of ye like   /   just sat there   /
smoked a feg   /   not a fuckin word   /   it's only now   /   i
understand now   /   fuckin pissed all the while   /   hard act
to follow   /   hard fuckin act to follow that   /   you givin it
nothin an her givin it all that   /   express yourself   /   get it
out to fuck   /   member the first gargle ya ever gave me   /
the starter   /   ma ma was away somewhere   /   just started
school a think   /   she was away an you give me a glass of
guinness   /   didn't say why   /   just gave me it an that was
that   /   the two lads havin a gargle   /   the two men   /   no
talk like just the gargle   /   wanna know somethin   /   i used
to admire that in you y'know   /   that silent thing   /   the
fuckin inner stuff   /   it felt   /   it felt like no matter what life
threw at ya or whatever   /   you just took it in yer stride   /
in yer stride   /   sort of thing   /   didn't mention that to you   /
didn't want to say anythin about it   /   wasn't that type of
effort   /   i'm sayin it now   /   it's not true now but i'm sayin
it now anyway   /   never said this before   /   this is between
me an you   /   you're not to fuckin use it   /   just talkin
y'know   /   understand   /   i could never make sense of ma
ma y'know that   /   no understandin a that   /   never fuckin
could get that one round ma head   /   couldn't   /   couldn't
get to the bottom of it   /   a know you know this by the way   /
but just in case ya   /   ya let it drift   /   see whenever   /
whenever ya wake up in the gutter   /   head on the fuckin
pavement   /   listenin to the rainwater movin   /   see the   /
the knowledge fairy comes down an fills yer napper with bits
a knowledge   /   you've been there   /   strange fuckin thing

that   /   you'd think ya get knowledge elsewhere   /   no   /
the gutter's the place for knowledge   /   learn somethin   /
(understand yourself)   /   can't   /   doesn't sort ya out
regardin other punters though   /   never the right type   /
i could never understand   /   this is the thing ya see   /   i
could never understand why she left   /   couldn't understand
why she just fuckin got up an left   /   a child   /   just a
fuckin child   /   nine   /   ten   /   eight   /   whatever   /
just left   /   thought she might've been here   /   not here
though   /   why did ma ma leave   /   oh very good   /
that's very good   /   cause she was a whore's melt fuckpot   /
a lot a use you are   /   i know   /   i fuckin know   /   ask
her   /   you   /   her   /   all the same like

KEVIN *gets one of the chairs and pulls it out into the*
*middle of the room. He indicates distance between the chair*
*and coffin.*

mother

*Addressing the chair.*

ya didn't hear that whore's melt thing there did ya   /   no   /
good   /   haven't seen this man in a while   /   understand
that   /   so   /   may have feelins about the situation   /
baggage   /   all that fuck   /   circumstances bein y'know   /
i'd prefer if the two of yous didn't go fuckin ga wha wha with
each other   /   the trick is to stay cool an talk shite   /   that's
the trick   /   right   /   be civil   /   the three of us   /   right   /
before   /   before we actually start   /   what about this   /
i think this is the way to go   /   apologise to each other   /
don't be gettin all fuckin up tight here   /   understand   /   i
fuckin know   /   reasons   /   you have reasons for not wantin
to   /   but i think it would useful   /   useful   /   enough said
/   right   /   men first   /   it's difficult   /   he can't   /   the
words are chokin him   /   you go first   /   no has to be him   /
come on da you can do it   /   get them out   /   deep breath
an away ya go   /   go on my son   /   did ya hear that   /
i heard somethin   /   he said it   /   there's it again   /   an
again   /   an again   /   an again   /   that's enough da fuck up
/   right you go   /   nothin to be sorry for she says   /   don't
start that shit   /   cool   /   calm   /   pretend if ya like   /

just say it   /   there ya go   /   do ya accept that da   /   you
fuckin pretend then   /   everythin's hunky dorey   /   grand   /
right   /   the crux   /   the crux of the matter   /   right

*Takes a drink.*

i   /   curious   /   i'd be curious   /   seein that   /   this
moment in time   /   that there's only the three of us   /   this
room   /   the three of us   /   our wee world type a thing   /
mother   /   father   /   child   /   right   /   that   /   that we
could sort of   /   a don't know   /   talk   /   that would be
my idea of what should happen   /   talk   /   just to speak   /
an   /   and maybe the situation   /   somethin fuckin   /
y'know   /   somethin good   /   somethin fuckin good might
happen   /   have be to capable of makin good happen   /
(right)   /   see here's   /   i'd like to know   /   back to the
knowledge thing ya see   /   see maybe   /   we can work
some circular   /   circle   /   things goin round an fuckin
round   /   go round in circles   /   might learn somethin   /
let's give it a go   /   i'd like to know   /   knowledge   /
whenever ya left   /   right   /   ma   /   whenever ya left   /
an i   /   i   /   see   /   i used to say to ma da why did ma ma
leave   /   he'd say   /   you'd say   /   cause she's a fucker
that doesn't care about us   /   that's why she left   /   right   /
now   /   that sort of   /   it's not workin so well now   /
alright   /   i'd like you to make some type of   /   explanation
/   i'd like you to   /   speak with   /   not just for me actually   /
not just for me   /   cause a mean   /   well he's dead now   /
y'know   /   but a mean   /   you   /   you   /   you could
fuckin   /   y'know   /   say to him   /   why did ya leave   /
cause she's a fucker that doesn't care about us   /   very good
da   /   i'm hopin ma   /   y'know   /   it's because of the
drinkin thing   /   i'm hoping that   /   cause   /   cause
there's somethin   /   there's somethin fuckin   /   there's
somethin tellin me y'know   /   that there wouldn't   /   i
wouldn't   /   i wouldn't like it to be cause you didn't care
about me   /   i wouldn't like to think that you left because of
me   /   i want to believe that you left because of him   /
what do ya say ma   /   it's him isn't it   /   yeah   /   that's a
good girl   /   it's him   /   he was a dirty drunken bastard   /
an you didn't like that sort of behaviour   /   so ya left   /   in

such a state you had to go   /   wild horses couldn't   /   aye   /
emotionally it was finished   /   i know   /   understandable   /
him no use cause of the drink an you tryin to make it work   /
needed away   /   not me though   /   not me sure it's not ma   /
you agree da don't ya   /   course ya do   /   no whore's melt   /
it's you   /   yes   /   excellent   /   that's that one sorted out   /
ya see   /   i'm happy about that type of notion   /   right   /
fille me with a calm   /   mi i me   /   ya understand   /   fill
of calm an ease   /   excellent   /   ya see   /   an now that
we're   /   now that we're talkin   /   talkin   /   we could   /
we could just   /   we could learn to be in some way fuckin
civil   /   ordinary   /   know what a mean   /   i don't know   /
yous two could sit round a table   /   maybe i could sit at the
table too   /   the three of us could sit round a table   /   we
could eat somethin   /   have a meal together   /   comfy   /
we could have a meal   /   an we could speak to each other   /
(we could talk)   /   we don't have to talk about anythin   /
y'know   /   anythin to fuckin deep   /   nothin mind fuckin
blowing   /   y'know   /   we could just sit round a table an
have a meal   /   a fry   /   breakfast   /   that's a good one   /
breakfast   /   yes that would be good   /   that's a date then   /
we'll do that   /   not now   /   not cookin fuck all now   /
fuck all to cook   /   afternoon   /   don't eat breakfast in the
fuckin afternoon anyway   /   tomorrow mornin   /   last meal
wha   /   get all dressed up   /   bit of a send off wha   /   ya
look well   /   what d'you think da   /   do ya think my mother
looks well   /   he thinks ya look well   /   for yer age   /   i
think she does too   /   the world's treated ya ok   /   has the
world treated you ok ma   /   yeah   /   yeah   /   looked after
ya alright didn't it   /   you look eh   /   yer garb   /   suits ye
y'know   /   good gear   /   good clothes   /   looks like ya
might've lead   /   happier   /   a better life   /   a happier life
than the two punters ya left behind   /   but   /   but then that   /
that would make sense   /   that would definitely make sense   /
you go you get rid of it   /   you stay it crawls into yer skin an
the rest   /   that   /   that   /   ya see   /   that again well   /
back to the knowledge thing   /   head on the pavement
knowledge fuckin fairy   /   (that's one of the   /   that's one
of the pieces)   /   fuck it   /   don't ya think she looks well   /
yes   /   you look well as well   /   ah   /   we all look well   /

to hell with it   /   why not say it   /   we're a lovely family   /
we   /   we   /   the three of us   /   we look fuckin brilliant   /
an   /   i'm lost for words   /   a mean if   /   never a fuckin
camera or photographer or whatever when ya need one   /
just the three of us here now   /   all dressed to kill   /   all
smile   /   picture   /   group photograph   /   y'know   /
i'm sure   /   there's somethin   /   i'm sure that there's one   /
us when we're all younger   /   haven't actually seen one   /
there's one there must be   /   can't really remember it bein
taken   /   but   /   took one on the sly aye   /   sleepin maybe
was a   /   we   /   we could compare the two   /   we could
put them up together on the wall   /   then an now y'know   /
black an white one   /   faded edges   /   an one all dressed in
our suits   /   lookin fuckin splendid

*He sits down beside his mother.*

bet you carried photographs around with ye   /   didn't ya   /
course ya did   /   no need to look at them now i'm here in the
flesh   /   ma ma wants to know da what it was like after she
left   /   concerned she is   /   do ya want to say somethin da   /
besides fuckin whore's melt   /   won't let that go   /   no go
no   /   i'll tell ya what   /   i'll speak an whenever you feel
the need just jump in there   /   right   /   good man   /   what
happened

*He laughs out loud – a false laugh.*

excuse me for laughin ma   /   this is funny to me   /   funny
but i don't know why   /   the story of what happened after
you fucked off   /   left   /   is a very simple one   /   nothin   /
nothin happened   /   fuck all   /   nothin   /   zero big time   /
life sort of continued on as it had been   /   no change   /
you just sat there old man didn't ye   /   where's ma ma   /
she's fucked off   /   end of story   /   how would ya explain
the way we were   /   how we got through the world   /   we
sort of just did our own thing   /   that's right our own thing   /
y'know   /   eh   /   a wee child an a grown man   /   not a
word   /   just did their own fuckin thing   /   that's what
happened   /   my ma says that she didn't think that's what
was goin to happen   /   no of course ya didn't   /   leave it
out   /   that's right   /   you're right   /   enough said   /

you know   /   you know   /   don't have to fuckin whatever
all the time   /   so   /   you were curious   /   well there you
go   /   i explained   /   whether ya thought that would happen
or not doesn't really fuckin interest me   /   i   /   i apologise   /
i'm sorry   /   y'know   /   i'd prefer if we didn't talk like this
/   keep things on a   /   i don't know   /   a friendly   /   a
palsy type of thing   /   y'know what a mean

*He takes a drink.*

(we just did our own thing)   /   didn't we da   /   that's it   /
continued on with his own life   /   watched him y'know   /
i left   /   i left da   /   didn't a leave   /   a did   /   a left   /
go an live in london oh yes   /   that was that   /   know what   /
yous might be interested in this   /   maybe not   /   maybe
not   /   might   /   might be interested cause i'm speaking   /
might have some type of interest in that notion   /   fuckin
strange   /   i found this   /   sometimes i'd be standin in a bar
/   talkin to people   /   y'know   /   ya just   /   ya talk to
them   /   can't remember if you're a talker or not ma   /   em   /
my da's not really much of a talker   /   understand what i'm
sayin   /   i'm talkin   /   findin out information   /   they're
asking ya information   /   things like   /   i don't know   /
anythin   /   work   /   family background an that   /   just
talkin   /   say somethin like   /   of the top   /   y'know   /
background information   /   haven't spoken to my da say in
fifteen years or somethin   /   same thing all the time   /
people   /   punters automatically assumed it was a big fallin out
affair   /   know what a mean   /   fuckin horrendous stuff   /
somethin really bad fuckin happened   /   all bad shit   /   no   /
nothin   /   a just left   /   haven't spoken since an that was
that   /   spend a life time talkin like that   /   every fucker the
same too   /   it could be   /   it could be like spouting off to
yourself at some stages y'know   /   ma's fucked off   /   da's
fuckin tortured   /   wife's left   /   children gone   /   that's
it   /   that's the one gets them   /   children gone   /   see it
in their faces   /   mean   /   rottin away   /   nothin to do but
fuckin wait   /   (nothin to do but fuckin wait)

*He takes a drink.*

good that we're gettin on like this   /   although ma   /   same
thing as my da earlier on   /   don't be thinkin for one fuckin
moment that   /   y'know   /   like that you're doin me a favour
bein here or fuck all   /   that's not what   /   we're just   /
we're havin a conversation   /   a civilised conversation   /
brighten dead arse up maybe   /   ha ha   /   what would
brighten my da up   /   just a wee bit   /   it's good   /   it's
good that yer here ma   /   this spirit of openness   /   that
type of   /   there's somethin you wanna say ma   /   mustn't   /
doesn't have to be personal   /   we'll understand   /   mighten
want to divulge too much   /   all a mean is   /   maybe   /
maybe ya could just   /   just tell us a wee bit   /   we could
work on that   /   wee bit   /   see   /   it's the   /   the clothes
/   the good clothes   /   get the chance   /   have to take the
chance   /   good times   /   nothin but good times   /   i think
/   you're right   /   that's all we need to know   /   we don't
know what we don't need to know   /   no more   /   not dead
/   not dead are you   /   no   /   no you're not dead   /   nah   /
hardly be wearing fuckin clothes like that if you were dead
would ye   /   not dead   /   (might weigh in)   /   wee woman
next door   /   you an her fight it out over the grief stakes   /
i like this   /   y'know   /   i haven't   /   haven't talked like
this   /   with people   /   don't know   /   for a long time   /
this is good   /   this is good ma   /   an da   /   isn't it   /
it's a fuckin belter   /   what's that da   /   you agree it's a
fuckin belter   /   thought ya might   /   good to talk   /
some days   /   some days i don't leave the room   /
outside's a fucker   /   eatin into your head   /   lookin   /
hours   /   lookin in the mirror   /   face   /   my face   /
me   /   get a blade cut my throat from ear to ear   /   deep   /
cut through it all   /   no bottle   /   fucker   /   get used to it   /
isn't that a real fucker chaps   /   sorry   /   too deep   /   i
understand   /   fuckin the atmosphere up   /   do yous wanna
know what happened to me   /   a mean   /   is it   /   do you
really   /   cause a mean if you don't   /   okey dokey   /
wouldn't like ya to feel ya were under a fuckin obligation to
yer offspring   /   d'ya know what a mean by that   /   y'know
/   if   /   if you're interested i'll say   /   but only if you're
interested   /   are   /   are   /   are you interested ma   /
yeah   /   an dead boy   /   interested   /   yeah

KEVIN *sits down.*

no verbals  /  make your mind up do-da  /  up an fucked
off  /  never thanked ya for the readies  /  day i was leavin
ma me da shook my hand  /  oh aye  /  good grip  /
shook my hand  /  says good luck  /  dropped me a tenner  /
a tenner  /  (big fuckin tenner  /  drank it)  /  ended up in
some boozer in fuckin kilburn  /  stayed there  /  didn't
move  /  stay put  /  nine aint with y.r own  /  plan was
to stay there for a wee while  /  earn some readies  /  come
back here  /  make life better for you  /  what a boy  /
that's not true da  /  wasn't ever comin back  /  both knew
it  /  didn't say fuck all that's all  /  kilburn  /  had to lay
bricks  /  look see  /  hands  /  look  /  brickie  /  not
now like  /  fuck that  /  done enough  /  not afraid of it  /
just fuck it  /  what i did  /  bricks  /  that's it  /  kip
flat  /  layin fuckin bricks  /  the woman in the flat  /
never met the woman in the flat

> KEVIN *stands up, walks to a chair, lifts it up and puts it in*
> *between his mother and his father. This chair is Theresa,*
> *Kevin's wife.*

alright  /  how's it goin  /  like my suit  /  belter  /
should tell the punters who you are  /  yeah  /  this is
theresa  /  theresa my  /  wife  /  women  /  fucked
off  /  i'm sorry theresa you should've met them under better
circumstances but things bein the way they are an me not being
god  /  ya takes your money an ya pays your chats  /
whatever it is  /  fuck it  /  can't remember  /  wanted
yous at the weddin by the way  /  i didn't think  /  not a
good idea  /  happy day  /  big happy day  /  couldn't
risk fuckin that up  /  couldn't risk fuckin that up theresa
sure we couldn't  /  no  /  understand that don't ya  /
thank you  /  i tell them how you an i fell in love will a  /
make them happy  /  yeah  /  layin brick  /  keepin ma
head down  /  few years  /  readies was good  /  nothin
happenin  /  just bangin away at it y'know  /  work most of
the week then round to the battle cruiser  /  round the corner  /
have a gargle then go home  /  that would be it  /  y'know  /
then from nowhere  /  from fuckin nowhere the lovely
theresa appeared  /  you appeared  /  a vision  /  blurred

vision   /   ha ha   /   two of us sittin there drinkin   /   talkin
/   good time   /   weren't they good times   /   the were   /
make each other laugh   /   didn't we make each other laugh   /
couldn't make ya laugh now   /   no   /   laughin   /   laughin
/   laughin   /   thought we'd get married   /   an we did

*Blows kisses to Theresa.*

(fuck this)   /   the women want to talk about the weddin day

KEVIN *lifts Theresa's chair and puts it beside his mother's.
He stands beside the coffin.*

want to have a word about things   /   probably have somethin
in common   /   this is like   /   this is like the way it should
be   /   the women on one side an the men on the other   /
what do ya think da   /   they could have a good natter an we
could just sit here an have a gargle

KEVIN *takes a drink.*

da do ya want a drink   /   a mean y'know   /   enjoy yourself
for fuck's sake

*He pours drink from the bottle over his father.*

there you go   /   god bless   /   look good   /   two a them   /
sittin there gabbin   /   used to make each other laugh   /   you
an ma ma make each other laugh   /   aye   /   course   /
beautiful   /   fuckin beautiful she was   /   wanted to come
here   /   never been here   /   live here like   /   get the
readies together come back here   /   settle

*Pause.*

don't be thinkin about that other thing   /   the blade effort   /
got fuck all to do with you   /   nothing to worry about   /
me   /   just me   /   forgot about it   /   just havin a drink
together that's all   /   the women   /   ok   /   say this is a pub   /
us standin at the counter   /   them down at the table   /   make
a good picture wouldn't it   /   good picture   /   sorry da   /
bustin to earrywig here   /   sorry da   /   later

KEVIN *sits down.*

(tired)

*He listens.*

is that the only question ya can think of askin   /   she left she
fuckin left   /   what   /   fuck both of yous   /   dummies
meeting   /   no speakin till i say so   /   it's not a good idea
da puttin them two together   /   no   /   funny types of
fuckers   /   talkin about ya   /   not a good idea   /   doesn't
serve any purpose y'know   /   talkin about ya   /   thinkin
un̶n̶u̶l̶ y̶u̶   /   m̶u̶u̶n̶g̶ u̶p̶   /   n̶n̶u̶r̶ m̶m̶g̶n̶ m̶v̶n̶m̶w̶n̶   /   m̶n̶g̶   /
shouldn't   /   (no thinkin about things)   /   isn't that right
theresa love   /   that's right love   /   that's right   /   this is
the time of celebration   /   we're all together for the first time
/   gargle   /   celebrates   /   good days ahead

*He takes a drink. Pours some over his father and waves the
bottle at the two chairs.*

there ya go   /   isn't that better   /   all able to look each
other in the eye now   /   all together   /   i think   /   i think
we should all talk about love   /   need to do that now   /   it's
time to do that   /   not that it matters a fuck but what do the
rest of yous think   /   who loves who   /   who says they love
who   /   for what fuckin reason does anybody love anything   /
this isn't goin to come as a fuckin earth shatterin dixie   /   i
don't love any one of the three of yous   /   you know that
anyway   /   there was a stage   /   but a mean   /   we grow
out of those things don't we   /   you wise up to yourself don't
ya   /   you realise it's not that type of a place   /   fuck it   /
why not lie   /   love yous for always   /   it's difficult to love
people when they're   /   never there   /   just fuckin pain
that's all   /   eat your insides up   /   fuckin chew them up   /
no time for it   /   no time   /   think we should try ma da's
way a thinkin   /   that's the best way   /   don't love anyone   /
can't get hurt   /   fuckin genius   /   yer a genius do you
know that   /   an absolute genius   /   don't mention it   /
ma ma doesn't agree with the genius thing   /   she doesn't
agree with the love thing   /   apparently there was a time da
when you loved   /   and someone loved you   /   but ya
fucked that up   /   would you like to   /   would you like to
expand on that   /   defend yourself   /   no ma he couldn't
that's right   /   nah   /   once there was a whiff of love in the
air an now it's just fuck all   /   nothin in the air   /   not even

a cool breeze    /    the air's fuckin solid as a rock    /    ach
well    /    the women's in agreement    /    sorted somethin out
the have    /    didn't take them long did it    /    insider info    /
readin from the same fuckin hymn sheet    /    talk among
yourselves there girls    /    need to ask my da somethin

*He bends down close to his father's head.*

what's    /    what's it like    /    the big leap    /    long sleep    /
a mean    /    are ya happy    /    i need you to say you're happy    /
the place you're in at this moment in time is a happy place    /
happy fluffy clouds    /    know what a mean    /    that everyone
was happy    /    that it was like    /    a better place    /    a
beautiful place    /    maybe snow    /    but it wouldn't be cold    /
not cold no    /    know what a mean    /    a place that was
better than the one ya just fuckin left    /    no cryin because ya
didn't know anybody    /    that would be a bad thing    /    a
very bad thing    /    all ya have to do is tell me it's a happy
place da    /    what d'you think    /    ya gonna tell me    /    do
that for me da    /    do that for me    /    good man    /    plenty
of ice cream    /    good man    /    ya hear that ma    /    a place
with plenty of ice cream    /    theresa    /    that be good    /
that be good wouldn't it    /    yeah    /    they wanna hear more
about me an you kid    /    wanna know the ins an outs    /
you tell them    /    alright i'll tell them but only because you
asked    /    better chance of the truth if you say    /    no fuck ya
i'll say    /    at the start    /    at the start it was the way things
should be    /    then it got better an better an better an better an
better an better    /    no    /    sank into a pit so deep that
nobody could see or hear a damn thing    /    that's very good    /
i'm very fuckin good    /    hidden talents dear    /    a pit so
deep ya couldn't see or hear    /    very good    /    ya think i
don't know things    /    i know fuckin plenty    /    the way it
worked out was    /    we used to both do the drinkin    /    have
a laugh    /    right down to the bottom of the bottle    /    fuckin
go baby go    /    always me more than her like    /    always me
more than you    /    yeah    /    two corners of the fuckin kip    /
glasses in hand    /    dull fuckin place    /    sittin there lookin
at each other    /    not a damn thing to say    /    no    /    i'm
sorry    /    i forgive you    /    nothin    /    not one word    /
see    /    it's the way things go    /    killin each other with a

stare   /   piercin right into your fuckin head   /   you realise   /
get that look   /   nothin you can do   /   not a damn thing   /
that right darlin   /   once that gaze's fixed everybody knows
the score all right   /   all leavin   /   we're all leavin   /
some walk an some float   /   how did you leave ma   /   did
ya walk or float   /   i didn't see ya   /   so   /   i assume ya
walked   /   a different type of a   /   a different type of a
fuckin thing connected with floatin   /   nah   /   what is this   /
what am i doin   /   fuck this nonsense   /   i don't even know
why i'm here   /   just sit here an have a drink   /   that's it   /
close your eyes a while   /   wake up   /   get everythin over
an done with an then get back home   /   walk back home   /
was your journey really necessary   /   what the fuck am i doin
here   /   somebody take me away   /   why doesn't the wee
woman from next door come in here   /   an just say go away   /
you're not wanted   /   a lot of fuckin nonsense   /   you
should have told me da   /   you should have give me the wire
about all this y'know   /   you fuck   /   wouldda made things
a bit   /   i'm spoilin the party am i   /   just when we're gettin
into the mood   /   spanner in the works   /   am i   /   i'd say
i was sorry   /   but   /   so fuck yous   /   not that i'm one to
apportion blame y'know but a mean   /   fuck yous anyway   /
(what is this   /   what is this)

*Drinking from the bottle.*

we should all try an be like the wee woman next door   /   i
think the world would be a better fuckin place for it   /   what
d'yous reckon

*Paces the room.*

what's wrong   /   what's wrong with yous   /   yous have
stopped talkin   /   a mean   /   yous have only met an yous
have stopped talkin   /   don't ya want to know what i'm like
ma   /   after all this fuckin time   /   don't ya want to know

KEVIN *faces the chair that is his mother and bends in close
as if telling a secret.*

this is for you too   /   your son   /   super fuckin duper
human bein   /   absolute belter   /   cares not a jot about

himself  /  lives only for others  /  he is without a shadow
of a doubt the most lovin carin gentle human bein ever born  /
my wife agrees  /  thank you theresa  /  very kind  /  ya
get all that  /  important that you got that  /  wouldn't want
ya to think while i've been away i've been wastin my fuckin
time y'know  /  i wouldn't want you to get the wrong
impression  /  too late for cryin now ma  /  wish ya had a
been about to see yer fine young son blossom into a fuckin
splendid adult  /  yeah yeah yeah  /  couldn't lend us
somethin could ya ma  /  few quid  /  score  /  help us
out  /  a gargle  /  y'know  /  yer wee son  /  a score  /
what's a score to a woman dressed like yourself  /  means
fuck all  /  score means nothin  /  an oul score for yer son  /
a score buys ya a lot of talk ya know that  /  bean-spillin type
of money that is  /  feel like sharing  /  group

*He pulls the chairs closer to the coffin – forms a group.*

comfy  /  wee bits at a time  /  brick by brick  /  get
there  /  won't we get there theresa  /  course we will  /
survivors  /  that's the name of the game  /  survivors  /
marriage darlin  /  difficult to tell with yous two but  /
y'know whenever ya get married  /  have this feelin  /  a
good feelin  /  deep  /  feelin it's gonna be alright  /  now
everythings gonna be swell  /  the fuckin thing that was
poundin in your head was gonna stop  /  found someone  /
found someone so it's gonna stop  /  no joke  /  felt that  /
a feelin  /  broke free or some fuckin thing y'know  /
killed the fucker that was in me y'know  /  my parent's son  /
you know all that theresa  /  i tell you that did a  /  no  /
well you know now  /  better late than never like  /  (stop
it  /  can't  /  come all this way)  /  can't switch off until
it's told  /  snow  /  lovely white snow  /  makes
everythin pretty  /  that would be a good idea  /  we'll do
that  /  ask god  /  ask the fuckin boyo to make it snow
tomorrow  /  everythin look lovely  /  what do ya reckon
boyo  /  can ya do that  /  click the figures  /  twitch the
fuckin nose or whatever it is you do  /  all fall down  /
blanket  /  white blanket

*Takes a drink.*

fuck the rest of you this time   /   don't know my form do
yous   /   theresa wants me to stop garglin now   /   could get
a bit hairy now y'know   /   card marked   /   been here
before   /   we've all fuckin been here before   /   either join
in darlin or fuck up   /   tell ma ma an da about the wall an the
room an everythin   /   fireplace   /   built a wall an a fireplace
an everythin   /   outside   /   outside now looked like a kip   /
a dirty fuckin kip   /   but inside a mean   /   it was lovely   /
It wasn't lovely   /   could've been lovely   /   when a say
built   /   that's right theresa thank you   /   correctin me   /
half-built   /   halfway there   /   not the full hundred yards   /
halfway fuckin there   /   job not completed   /   the point is
da   /   you should have wired me off   /   you should have
let me know that at some stage things could go a bit fuckin
wrong   /   that the picture inside yer napper wasn't always the
one that stays with ya   /   the one ya first have y'know isn't
the one that stays there   /   it can be   /   it can be a different
type of fuckin picture   /   you should have wired me off about
that   /   i'd a done that   /   a child of mine   /   yes   /
wired them off   /   that life mightn't be rosy for them   /   i'd
a done it   /   son   /   what was it like ma to hold me as a
baby   /   was it a good feelin   /   was it   /   wrap me up in
a towel after the bath   /   that's a good feelin isn't it   /   to
look at your child   /   to look at its eyes   /   an think that it's
perfect   /   to think that that's the way the world should be   /
an that's the way it is for them   /   the comfort of their
mummy's arms   /   nothin there to block the sun out   /
theresa doesn't like you ma d'ya know that   /   never did   /
she wants to know   /   how you could have walked out on
your own child   /   in order to walk out on your own child
you'd need to be some type of a scumbag fuckpot to do that   /
that the phrase you're thinkin about theresa   /   that's the
phrase ma   /   scumbag fuckpot   /   shouldn't stop the two of
yous bein good friends though   /   outside was a fuckin kip   /
a dirty fuckin kip   /   have to go   /   not for your ears   /
say bye bye   /   some other time

   *Pushes Theresa's chair over.*

just between us   /   me   /   all me

   *Takes the suit off and throws it away.*

the real me  /   the me  /   the delightful fuckin me  /   look
/   this is it  /   this is what  /   this is me  /   think you
know me  /   ya know fuckin nobody  /   fuckin kip  /
two of us used to gargle the bit out y'know  /   didn't  /
didn't bother goin to the pub anymore  /   get used to doin
things the way ya fuckin do them that's all  /   kevin  /
(kevin)  /   that was a  /   that was her idea  /   theresa  /
liked the name  /   i hate the fuckin name  /   fuckin hate it  /
my name  /   not yer name son  /   my name  /   all called
kevin  /   that right da  /   fuckin  /   i don't know  /   this
is my way  /   my way of sayin yous are grandparents  /
wee boy  /   wee kevin  /   kevin the boy child  /   drinkin
the fuckin bit out  /   made a pact  /   a deal  /   should
make fuck all  /   never tell the devil too much of your mind
wha  /   a deal  /   when the baby  /   (when the baby)  /
it was all gonna change  /   no more gargle  /   only right  /
right fuckin thing to do  /   sacrifice  /   make a fuckin
sacrifice  /   do the right fuckin thing  /   listenin to this
grandparents  /   are the grandparents listenin  /   the world  /
the world  /   fuckin kip  /   people no good  /   no fuckin
good  /   liars  /   fuckin liars  /   two fuckin liars  /   for a
while  /   worked out for a while  /   couldn't  /   couldn't
make it the way  /   tried to be good  /   did  /   want you
to believe that  /   finish things  /   the house y'know  /
never fuckin finished anythin  /   dirt  /   fuckin dirt  /
nothin will happen  /   nothin happens  /   that's what was
said  /   few drinks end of the day  /   relax  /   kevin  /
wee kevin  /   never spoke  /   never spoke  /   don't know
what it was  /   nobody fuckin knows  /   i know  /   he's
crawlin around the place  /   we're back into the gargle  /
shoutin  /   screamin  /   sees that didn't want to speak  /
fuckin kip  /   know the way da  /   know the way garglin
early in the day can be good  /   everybody goin about their  /
doin whatever it is they do  /   not in  /   just standin off a
bit  /   wee drink gives it all a better edge  /   put it out of
focus  /   just enough to get it all wrong  /   hear that  /   to
get it all fuckin wrong  /   night before fuckin crazy  /
drinkin  /   me an her into it  /   woke up  /   the place is
all everywhere  /   nothin ever fuckin changes  /   sittin
early mornin havin a drink  /   she's still in bed not be up for

hours  /  fuckin kip  /  kevin wakes up  /  lift him out of
his cot  /  soakin  /  nobody changed him all night  /
full  /  drunk  /  didn't change him  /  it's cold  /  have
to keep him warm  /  snowin  /  everythin's covered in
snow  /  looked beautiful  /  looked like a place  /
looked like another world  /  another place  /  not the one
we were in  /  another one  /  a nice one  /  wanted kevin
to see that world  /  couldn't speak  /  see another world  /
a nice world  /  a warm world  /  had to keep him warm  /
give him a hug  /  not you son  /  not happen to you  /
i'll protect ya  /  keep ya warm  /  a big hard hard hug  /
put him back in his cot  /  white blanket over him  /  keep
him warm  /  wee angel  /  snow  /  better place  /
have another gargle

*Silence.*

what  /  nothin to say about that

*Pause.*

fuck yous  /  not like i fuckin need any of yous  /  don't
need no fucker  /  just leave  /  all yous are fuckin good for
is leavin  /  no fuckin time to look at people

*Shouts into coffin.*

understand  /  understand people  /  didn't try  /  didn't
give a fuck  /  why didn't ya wire me off  /  fuckin tell me

*Punching the body.*

why didn't ya fuckin tell me  /  fuck  /  fuck  /  fuck

*He stops punching – pauses – touches his father's face.*

i'm sorry  /  sorry sorry sorry sorry sorry  /  here

*Pours drink over the father's face.*

good luck  /  should've  /  sorry ma  /  sorry  /  all fuckin
/  y'know  /  sorry  /  good  /  good talkin like that  /
(talkin)  /  i'm tired  /  y'know tired  /  have to lie down  /
lie down

*He lifts his mother's chair and puts it in the coffin.*

wee sleep  /  that's better  /  wee sleep

*He lays on the ground beside Theresa's upturned chair. He holds the empty bottle close to him.*

fuckin cold    /    cold

*He covers himself with his father's overcoat, attempts to get comfortable.*

fuckin chair's too hard    /    get some good chairs    /    don't need no fucker

*He closes his eyes.*

wee woman    /    next door    /    lovely wee woman    /    look after me    /    look after me

# BRAZIL

Ronan O'Donnell

*For Lesley*

*Brazil* was first presented by Kate McGrath for Theatre of Imagination at the Latchmere Theatre, London, on 11 February 2003 and subsequently at The Arches, Glasgow, on 9 April 2003, with the following cast:

DODDY                              Anthony Strachan

*Director*   Graeme Maley
*Designer*   Louise Anderson
*Lighting Designe*   Maria Bechaalani
*Composer*   Brian Docherty
*Stage Manager*   Phil Hewitt

With thanks to James Cunningham

**Character**

DODDY

*Somewhere in the Central Belt (Scotland). A derelict space
near or on a peripheral housing estate. Lights up on* DODDY.
*A voice-over flickers into life, the News:*

NEWS. A spokesperson said . . . (*Static.*) The European
Federation warned the US this morning against any escalation
of the trade war and specified that it should withdraw its forces
from Mungotown by tomorrow or face the consequences.
Attacks have been going on all day. (*Static.*)

   *Megastore.*

DODDY. The Marmite . . . The lid's off. Clocked security
guards and that young manager at the other end o the store.
Practising the company song, know? Pure knobsters, know?
A row o blue jumpers chanting out how the company is . . .
'magic'. Knobsters, know? If a was on camera chances are a
wizny being watched. Chances are there wiz wall tae wall
screens. Fuzzy screens. Snowy screens. An peepers meant to
be clockin the bold yin here, would be focused elsewhere . . .
on a ham sandwich . . . or on a young mum's wiggle mair like
– arse chewing dainties. An the hamshanker in the control
room, know? On his ownieo. Giving it over the radio tae his
pals on the floor:

'Guess who's in the shop? In the biscuit aisle. Checking oot
the Jammy Dodgers? Bent er. Blonde that looks like lap dancer
Amber. Mind the staff night out, up the Pubic Triangle? The
strut fluff.

Want tae get ma bar code oot, baby doll?' That's the kind o
cunts they ur. My old man used to be wan, before his veins got
clogged and he got whacked wi a baseball bat for a ton o scrap
copper. Ma pals did that. Ma so called sod brothers. Spent half
his life in front o a security screen. Reading *True Detective* and
pullin his duff tae dirty books.

So . . . dig this. The lid's off. Am sticking my fingers in, right
in, but the Marmite's no have'n it. Then a sees a wee woman

pushin a disability trolley – so a goes intae ma smother-up routine. She totters by wiout a second glance. Am just this short-sighted bam goggling the label fur vitbits, rubbin ma chin like am really intae the jar's genetical compounds – so to speak.

The old doll's by. A right twitcher, a dribbler, an empty bungalow. The occupier skidaddled many moons ago, know? In her front parlour the wheel's turnin but the hamster's deed, know? So ma digit's in the jar an am just about to scoop a blob o the black gear intae ma gub when – cop for this – 'Just grazing, are we, sir?' That young manager's at ma shoulder. 'Just enjoying the buffet, are we, sir?'

Where'd he come from? 'Got a sudden attack of the munchies, sir?' He's meant to be up the back practising the company song wi the other knobsters. He looks me up and down. A deeks him. A baldy blonde, full o young puke. His tie's patterned wi cartoons.

The blob wiz between us. A watched it sag aff the end o ma fingers towards the ad staring up at us frae the polished floor. Caught bonnie! A has a daft idea to deface his smug jug wi it. Maybe smear it all oe'r ma own face. But I clocked in his visage that staff mag look – they're mad for his manager's specials at HQ, know? He's always been keen on pie charts. The rise and fall o the blancmange, that's what curls his toes. I didny want a scene:

'Alright, fair enough. It's only a bit o Marmite, know?'

'Would you step this way, sir – to the office.' That's what he says. Smug jug. I could tell he was a gym bunny.

A knows all about 'the office.' At the far end o the store is the holding pens. The corridor wi bars on it. That's the 'office'. There'd be three or four tea-leafs sitting in there already. I've been there before. The screws were waiting also – Big Betty and Double Bubble. Human grease on the ancient cuffs, know? I'm on the conveyer belt and a can feel the hot lamp o the medic checkin ma baws for crabs. The thing wiz to maintain yer dignity between here an there, whilst you're still a civvy, a standard shopper. That's the important bit. Whilst you're still

wearing the regular clobber, no they arse rags. See the gear
they make you wear? Dread yer first untried visit. The shoes
that are boats. Insoles hard and shiny-worn like a passage
buffed in stone. An the stylish jacket made frae mole. A
uniform a hundred years old. Lag hole after lag hole next tae
yer skin makes it itch, know? Fuck, loud and clear, a can hear
my number being chalked up on the dog-box door.

4-2-7-1. Scratchy chalk.

Strutting towards the holdin pens at the back o the store . . .
trying tae swagger – trying to swagger   the floor beneath us
turns tae sponge. The world wobbles an I get the wobblies.
Hardly put one foot in front o the other. Like when it's
summer, beautiful summer, the tarmac melts, an yer trainers
stick. I'm tellin yi. Gum-steps. The special offers are spinning
round and round. Been here before, know?

I tried to tell him . . . the baldy blonde . . . wi the heed full o
blancmange, to stop screwing the cuff o ma jacket into a knot.
Tae get his hands off. It wiznny necessary. I'm being
cooperative. I know the score. You'll get your Brownie points.
Let's walk normal. A told him time an again. But aw naw, he's
a fuckin gym bunny . . .

I can see shoppers looking round. Dirty looks, know? Like
they've spotted a steaming tolly amongst the croissants, nearly
touched it wi their precious mitts. Lookin at uz the way fiscal
sneers at juvenile defendant in oversized tin flute.

So I gubs him – a has tae. Nae choice. Two digs . . . rapido! An
a penalty kick . . . in the solar plexus. Dig that oot the back o
the net, know? Just to keep him decked for the few but vital
seconds a needs to disappear, know? Vanish. I'm no here. You
don't see me, happy shoppers, OK? The old witness
statement's a blank page. Yer affidavit's bum roll, know? I'm
off oot o here!

A looks back before a turns the corner and he's lying there,
smug jug, the gym bunny, in the foetal position, very still. An
this couple, in his-an-her red jumpers, are bending over,
peering at him like he was at the bottom o the sea. Like he's a
curio in the fish tank amongst the plastic reeds.

I didny panic – didny run. Might be wan o they have-a-gos about. Blow you oot yer Calvin Kleins. A walks quickly to the exit. Confusion crackling behind me. The hamshanker in control's pushing buttons. Canny push enough fuckin buttons. I can hear boots skidding behind me as security takes the corners.

I'm through the doors an sprinting. My face breaking air the way jet pilots' coupons go. An this Black Thing's at ma back, snatching at ma flapping jacket! . . . The Black Thing, know? Always wi me. Fate or somethin. Wearing shades, know? Sniggering. Always turns up tae oversee the disaster scene. When I got carted for the first time – it was there. The Black Thing. When the Wee Men got me beneath the stadium an kicked ma melt in, it was there. When I was coming back frae the back green bog in the dark after *Don't Watch Alone!* It was there, know? Some things yer born wi, know? This Black Thing's like a twin. But I hivny got a twin. That bad . . . That fuckin heavy, know?

I'm sprinting across the car park telling myself never again. This is the last time. I'll never slacken again, promise. A runs like fuck tae the perimeter fence. Scrambles through a hole. Wan I'd prepared earlier, know? Rolls down the embankment – oot o sight. Hides in scrawny bushes. Ma heart's poundin . . . It's a long time before I stops panting. Then the only lug-notes . . . the only lug-notes . . . sounds . . . ur the countless plastic bags snared in the woods round the megastore. Logos aw at different stages o decomposure, know?

I gets a hard-on . . . A gets a hard-on lying in yon ditch. All am doing is looking at the sky through bare sprigs. Licking Marmite frae ma fingers . . . an a gets a stiffie. I'm thinking, ma meat's no right. Wit's this fuckin trunk swelling in ma breeks? Wit's goin on here? I whips it out an looks at it – looks at it a long time. Stumped? Amazed? I don't know which. I've met this beast before. It says zilch. Truth is ma tadger feels fuckin older than me. It's a stane-pecker! . . . A geez it 'the God's Bless'. I geez the tadger the sign o the Dirty Beast, know?

*Makes the sign of the cross over his hard-on.*

*The Dumps.*

The rubbish dumps. I'm up here nearly every day. Vast mouldy heaps. Like overnight a whole city's been dismantled. Like a doolie-doomster breenged through a million streets. A million rooms sucked into its gurgling guts, know? Nobody comes here. Tae scavenge. The past is taboo – mair than useless. They garbled heaps only remind folk of what's sanctioned. I treat it like a job, finding things. Odd things like piles o comics. Boxes o torn photos. The hub cap frae a Cadillac. Bust o a grandee, wan o they digiridatari dudes. I'm ey shufflin the stuff about – but it canny . . . it canny be fitted into any kind o order. Sometimes at night I feel sad an the object am lookin at makes oonoo, know? It doesny last.

A seen this programme wance. About how they found the Temple o Solomon. Found it in Ethiopia. Dug it up frae this ancient rubbish dump and inside hunders o arks – arks right, know? Different sizes and shapes an all empty. Arks all empty, know? They reckon the nomads hiv got it, know? The wan that isny empty. It's carted about strapped tae the back o this holy coo. I dinny believe a word o it – there's nae such thing as a story . . . On ma wall, know? I've pinned up this fully illustrated double-page spread – when the terrorists wiped oot the governments. High Heed yins all charcoaled. Motorcades blown tae bits. I don't know what it says – cos I canny read. There's a photo of Commander X. The Gaffer. Ma wee sister reads. She sits on ma bed an practises wi the colour charts. Me holdin the torch. Nomadic Glow, that's number 21. Purple bing . . . that's number 57. Orinoco broon . . . 88/A. Banana Dream, 99. Lusty Lavender – her favourite . . .

I'm sitting . . . Am sitting blowing smoke rings on a scrap motor, know? When who comes stoating along the path but ma sod brother, Cockroach. Bowley legs he's got – short arms and the longest Mars bar you've ever clocked. Here tae here, it is.

*Mars bar/scar runs from his brow to chin.*

Like his grin's been switched to vertical . . . I seen him wance – his legs embedded in this skinny guy's belly, his fingers locked round the guy's guzzle. Taking liberties – again. That's his style. A true sod brother. We get on well but the pupils o his eyes shrink tae the size o pin heads when I nearly says 'Cockroach' tae his face. Ma mistake. He doesny like that handle. His name's Gary, I think. Or Darren . . . maybe. He takes the fag from between ma lips. Has a drag. 'The German army's landed. 30,000. Tanks an that.'

*Silly spits.*

That's what he does after every statement.

*Silly spits.*

We debates the ins an outs o it, the Krauts landin. How the war's going. 'A want to be a tank commander. Gee the Yanks a doin!'

*Silly spits.*

I suggest he come home wi me for his tea. He leaps at the chance – he fancies ma wee sister, see. 'Is she gonny be there?'

*Silly spits.*

'I think so.' 'Is she gonny be there?'

*Silly spits.*

Asks a million times. Does this fuckin stupid slippery jig. His jug is beetroot. He's lookin round for a nosegay to charm her wi. He's done it before, but it's no that time o year an there's only icicles, know?

*Super Screen.*

We takes a donner. A donner on doon the road. Ma Ma an Da are sitting in the living room watching the super screen. Super screen takes up half the room. It dissects a corner, know, an behind it is where stuff is tossed. Any old shite. You get used to the ming. There's a pair o crutches behind the telly. I've never figured oot the crutches, who ditched them there?

They hiv the temerity to have wan o they screen enlargers stuck on the front o the telly. A lens tae increase the intensity o the picture even further. Hyper it, screw it right intae yer brain-pan, know? The screen enlarger, wan leg's buckled so it's lopsided – the picture's skewed so the whole family watches the telly like that . . .

*Head resting on left shoulder.*

Sitting there on the sofa like a bunch o plums, know?

Da's intae gadgetry, an the fag catalogues are stacked neatly by the side o the sofa. The wan on top o the pile's opened at the latest range of snooping devices. Da's saving up for this thing that sees through walls. Straight up. Her next door's on the game. You can hear the punters sometimes. Faraway shouts. 'G'on, ma laddie! G'n, ma laddie! That's ma laddie!' Like guys shoutin on their whippets. The old man canny wait to see through that wall. You see him lookin at it. He's got a piece of wallpaper peeled back like an Elastoplast, exposing the raw brick. Maybe she's already got a device and she's lookin at uz in our goldfish bowl. Bet she is. Bet she's lookin, right now . . .

President Klintnick is on the super screen. Dead jovial in wrap-around sound, wi his jutting chin. Like, if he walked in the pub it would be: 'Hey guys, long time, no see. See the bevvy, the bevvy's on me!' Right you are, know? Pure knobster.

Klintnick's stonnin in front o his flow chart – in short sleeves. Laughing at his own quips. Going on about how the plants in Maryland and Chicago are still producing too many dud bombs. Dud fuckin bombs! Tell that to fuckin Mungotown!

'The German army's landed, there'll be plenty jobs,' ma Da side-swipes it snidy.

'Nae jobs for you, ya'n old scrot,' I'm thinking. 'All that's left for you is lotto and torn hole.'

Ma Ma's yanking ma sleeve. 'Did you get ma Marmite? Did you get ma Marmite, son, did yi?' 'No I didny get yer fuckin Marmite.' She's all Smeagolly, wringing her hands.

She sits there all day cemented into blue fluffy slippers. She says her prayers in them, sleeps in them, shuffles to the lavvy in them. You can follow her trails in the linoleum. The most well-worn path leads straight to the pill cabinet.

'Geez the God's Bless, son. I don't know wit road to go doon. Geez the God's Bless! A need it now.' Her teeth loose in her pink mooth. So a gee her the sign o the Dirty Beast – a quickie, know?

*Makes the sign of the cross.*

Ma Da's wound up. Braw. He canny stand her sprinkle o holy
water. 'Doesny matter wit hope. The shit's total!' That's his
usual script. He speeds it intae ma lug. Yak. Yak. Yak. Sitting
there, getting off on his own bile. Is that wit A'm gonny grow
intae? That fuckin horror story sitting on the sofa? Puffed up in
his pig billet. I get an urge to punch him. There's something
between us, know, me an ma old man, that isny there.

I need fresh air, know, but the old Maw's on her knees,
blocking the doorway. 'Mon son, it's time tae say yer prayers.
Mon son.' If a can help it a dodge this bit but looks like there's
nae escape the day.

DODDY *kneels.*

Ma Ma gets doon on her knees a couple of times a day. Round
about this hour she has a wee session. Me and ma Ma and
sometimes ma wee sister, kneel the gether. We turn the telly
down, Da sits muttering fucks. Chant our God's Bless. You just
make it up like as you go along, know? Whatever comes into yer
heed. Ma Ma starts the ball rolling. Her eyes are all screwed up
. . . 'Our Doddy . . . Our Doddy. Who art beyond . . . who art
beyond . . . er . . . er . . . ' She's no on form the day, eh? She
struggles for words. A carry on. 'Who art beyond the fog
midden. Puddle mingle. Couldny give a fuck. Indifferent.' Ma
Ma likes it so far, she's nodding her heed rapid. The old man
storms out the room, pushing the old dear aside. I shout after
him: 'Give us our will to pursue our pleasure and it tae drink
us as drunk is drank by drink!' The old dear is off now as she
joins in: 'Be we gauzy torn by May-gobs . . . frail as I am wi
nae nest . . . er . . . eh.' 'Forgive us nowt,' says I. 'As it will all
be done again and again. In short order say *aye*. Cos aye tae
wan solo joy means all torn holes get the thumbs up. Even as
I fuckin plod on, against nae freedom, yet quest . . . pro . . . tec
. . . ted.'

'Hinging by a wee thread son,' ma Maw says. 'Hinging by a
wee thread, Doddy.' Then her slobbers over ma mitts as she
kisses my knuckles wet. 'Thank you son, thank you son. Thank
you son!' She turns me off. 'Why do you always embarrass
me, Maw? Get aff yer knees! Get yer lips off!' 'Don't tell yer
Da,' she whispers it, slipping me a couple o pills. 'The big blue

yin's best son.' She winks it. 'Mind, the big blue one. Don't tell yer Da.' I looks into her glaikit eyes and canny suss the why. Maybe it's the pills? Maybe it's the God's bless? She geez it glee when she's had a good spirit session.

*He makes the sign of the cross.*

A finds the sod brother in the lobby peering through the lavvy door at Margaret in her undies. She's wearing a turban o soap bubbles. 'She's got some tits.'

*Silly spits.*

He says it like it's an awesome piece o skill to see a pair o boobs flannelled, know? 'She's really nice.'

*Silly spits.*

His jug's went beetroot. Maggie kicks the door shut but it just bounces open again and we stand watching her for the few tries it takes to finally slam it in our gawking gubs . . .

I know where Cockroach is coming from. A do. There's something . . . dead certain . . . That's it. Something *certain* in every move o her body. She glows it right beautiful. Beautiful that's stronger than strength. No like ma thumbles. Am bushwhacked by all sort o things, tin openers, umbrellas. Born to be nutmegged, know?

'Fancy a pint?'

*Silly spits.*

Cockroach mumbles it, tugging me away frae the door. 'Doddy, fancy a pint? Your wee sister's brand new, know? She's brand new. Brand new.'

*Silly spits.*

*The Goody Two-Shoes.*

Me an Cockroach set off to visit the local pub. Ma's at the windy. Waving. Am fingerin the big pill in ma pocket. It's the only pub in a scheme o ninety thousand: The Goody Two-Shoes. It has five floors and is painted pink. It has all sorts o theme sections. Wan zone where you can listen to Elvis all day. In another it's New Bottle an Plastic Jumper. Nostalgia, know?

To get there we have tae get past Fat Tongo though. The streets are designed tae segregate. The Wee Men frae The Boot Boys. The Boot Boys frae The Young Mental Team. Young Mental Team frae Spur Ya Bass! There's only two ways in or oot o the entire scheme. The CCTVs controlled by disabled googlies, the Daleks, know? They get their windies panned. Dog shit smeared on their door handles.

Fat Tongo would be in his front garden as usual, guaranteed. Sitting on a mouldy sofa wi the telly blaring through the windy. A drum o homemade hooch beside him. He'd have his air rifle at the ready, the ball bearings in his mouth. It's no so much the gun as his twelve Dobermans that hiv free rein o the street. Straight up man, know. It's gen. The corner where his tenement is situated is littered wi dog turds.

We gets there an sees Tongo peering over the hedge. The fat bastard's stonnin – balancing on the edge o the sofa – there's a commotion at the far end o the street. His dogs have caught something, know? A few neighbours are spectating frae their windies, there's dull applause, know? It's a lucky break, but as we're sneaking by this old windy-hinger on the top storey spots us and shouts a warning to Fat Tongo, know? 'There they ur, Tongo. There they ur, two Tagues, two Fenians. Dinny let the mingers get away, son.' For a moment he doesny know whether to shoot or whistle up his Dobermans. We're running. I know a cul-de-sac wi a high fence we can climb over. Tongo's rapid fire is sniping leaves frae the hedges round our heeds. Laurels fur the numptees, know? Cockroach is shouting, spitting oot fuck-words like he's returning tennis baws, know? 'You're as thick as shit mixed wi porridge!' That sort of stuff. 'Yer auld maw's a cow's cunt!' A pellet pierces the lob o Cockroach's ear. Another pops a hole in his neck. We reach the fence. I shin it. I look back at him, his pupils have almost disappeared. He's frozen meat, fingers hooked intae the chain link. A climb back an wi ma shoulder under his pissy arse heave him over, know? Just in time as Tongo's pack of mutts are leaping at the fence. I pick up a stick and gee the snarlers a wee stir. Poke the stick through the chain link. Get that doon yer gub, chew this! Chew it! Three of them have got it and they're no letting go. They're no letting go. Get that doon yer gub!

*Doocot.*

Runnin for ages – sees a doocot – hide in it. Get our breath
back. This wan's made o corrugated sheets, clapboard, painted
black. Tall like a rocket. It's got 'Wee Men Ya Bass' sprayed
on its sagging tube. We're in Wee Men territory. Got to keep
the edge up, know? Inside it smells o feathers an wet wood.
Rows and rows o doos in cages. We has a fag. I blow ma
smoke through wan o the holes in the corrugated metal. Ignite
engines! Blast us tae fuck oot o here! All Cockroach can yak
about is the red-bar-starry doo strutting on a ledge above his
heed. A huge pouter. 'Look at that. That's all A want to be . . .
is a pouter like him or a tumbler. Clap wings, Doddy!

*Silly spits.*

A want to be that red-bar-starry doo. So a do.'

*Silly spits.*

He's gone pure peely wally and he's forgotten about the blood
dripping frae his torn lug and neck, know? He starts to mutter
about Maggie, ma wee sister. Maybe it's the doo's bill and
cooing but he says . . . about her, 'our roots are intertwingled,
Doddy.'

*Silly spits.*

I think that's what his whisper is? Keeps wisping it, 'Our roots
are intertwingled.'

*Silly spits.*

'Shut up you . . . There's a Doberman sniffing about the doocot
. . . You want tae gee the game away?' I prefer it when he's got
nothing to say. When he talks vital it reminds me too much o
ma own pretend. If folks could see ma pretend they'd cry me a
liar.

*The Malky.*

We finally get up the hill to The Goody Two-Shoes. The
council dumps tower above it – I persuade Cockroach to try
the silent bar. There's hardly anyone in, no music an the
barman's neck's craned towards this mute telly. Pictures o the
German army. A bands man wi roses round his helmet and folk

flinging confetti. He's puffin intae this fat – shiny thing. Spud is sitting wi Bob Blunt boozing. Aw naw! Bob Blunt is a knobster to be avoided. His real name's actually Bob Sharp but he's a fat know-all, a pub-quizmeister . . . so everybody calls him Bob Blunt. Then we clock The Malky, Cockroach's Da is at the other end o the bar on his tod an the sod brother starts to sort of shiver. 'It's no your lucky day, is it?' He's shit scared o his old man. Into my mind cartwheels the tale Cockroach telt o the time The Malky tries to catch a bluebottle. They're in the house, the whole family, watching the telly after supper and The Malky's bugged by this buzzing pester that seems to be specially attracted tae his left lug. So The Malky cracks up. Goes for it wi a rolled up mag. The Granny's shouting 'calm doon son', he's breaking things see. Crunching family nick-nacks under his tartan slippers. Then there's a power cut. The whole street's zoned oot. Does that deter The Malky? No danger! In the pitch dark he's still after the buzzing pester, trashes the fuckin place in short order. He's tangled in the curtains. He's knocked the old yin oot her comfy chair. Tears her nighty. Dishes out a few black eyes. Finally puts the coffee table through the windy. Some tiff that, eh? That's Cockroach's Da. An he's over there fu o drink.

The Malky never talks to anyone, speaks wi his peepers, two holes pissed in snow. Now he spots us ordering our pints. The Malky is saying something – looking right at me. I've never ever heard the guy utter a single word. Even the barman stops what he's at. He says it quietly an only once frae the other end o the shop, pointing at his boy . . . but lookin at me. 'He's . . . no . . . wan . . . o . . . mine. Ge'uz the God's Bless.' So a gee the tadger the sign o the Dirty Beast, know? Gez him a double dose fur good measure. A turns round an Cockroach is bomb vapour, offski, only spots o blood on the floor tiles.

So I'm sitting wi two pints, in pint nirvana, watching the German army kissing old ladies and throwing sweets at weans. I clock Bob Blunt is shifting in his seat, busting wi answers to unasked questions. He's signalling to me. The old pub semaphore. Ignore him. He's trying to tell me a gag. That's what he's trying to do. A pregnant cow, right? Got that. Goes on a week's holiday, right? I nod my heed. She has a wee calf,

right? A wee calf?? Thank fuck it's a silent bar. I turn back tae
the telly and the German army mobbed by weans. The camera
pulls back an a recognise the bridge they're marching over.
Under it flows a working river. No like ours which skulks
through the burnt bingyards. Ponging sludge, know? The
cooncil are considering paving it over. The river on the telly's
crammed wi cranes an that, know? A think o years to come an
our river, an me, an old yin, lifting up a stank and climbing
doon on the metal rungs into the darkness . . . Just to listen.
I fancy that.

*Rust.*

I neck ma pints. A suss where ma sod brother has shifted an a
climb up through the tyres an mattresses, tae where the scrap
motors are aw stacked, aw sea colours, briny. I love rust. It's
ma favourite colour an it's everywhere. It covers the roofs o the
scheme. It just takes a certain kind o light to pick it oot, then it
glows, know?

Up here you can see the whole scheme. Cockroach is wanderin
about. He stops, stares at the piles o mingle mangle. 'Where's
it come frae, Doddy?'

*Silly spits.*

It comes from everywhere, man. 'Where it come frae, Doddy?'

*Silly spits.*

He toes into the air an auld chime piece. He's dolly dimple . . .
I goes to where am working, excavating this plaster angel.
Must be frae a chapel. A Fenian joint. Underneath the grime
the angel's actually pure black like coal an she's holdin a wean
an I'm wiping her face clear wi spittle. Know her face? It's no
angelic at all. Ma Ma's angelic cos she's an eejit, an all she
wants is Marmite. Angel's eyes are hooded, carnal. It's the face
o a woman who understands cock. The face o a woman who's
been loved and probably hawked it, know? And the wean's
face – it knows too.

She reminds me o a piece o verse ma Da recites on Burns
Nights when the whole scheme parties and the hooch is

everywhere. It's his only party piece an the only time he
blubbers it.

Wantonness for evermair . . .

That's it . . .

Wantonness his been ma ruin,
Yet for aw my dool and care
It's wantonness for evermair.
I hae loved the Black, the Brown
I hae loved the Fair, the Gowden.
Aw the colours in the toon
Wantonness has been my ruin.

I geez the angel the God's Bless. A geez her and the wean the
sign o the Dirty Beast.

*Mister President.*

So, I'm workin away, frae the waist down the angel thingy's
trapped in wires an other garbage. A've tain my jacket off an
I'm pishin sweat when a hears Cockroach howlin. He's jumpin
up an doon on the roof o this rust bucket, pointing. I climb up,
an at first I canny understand. 'Wit's the score wi you? Talk
fuckin sense, will yi!' All he can say is, 'Doddy . . . Doddy . . .
monster!'

*Silly spits.*

He's got a clump of his own hair in his fist, as if he's trying to
lift himself off the deck. His words become spit. He's about tae
take a burn oot. Time tae shift. But then I see wit's agitatin
him. Midges . . . a swarm o . . . bees or somethin, that just
keep getting bigger an bigger . . . An we watch as the side
winders smack intae our scheme . . . The explosions are bright
red and the blasts are flipping roofs off. Tiddlywinks wi whole
streets . . . o people. Yer thinking this is only meant tae happen
on the news. I'll wake up in a mo. In a mo I'll look oot the
bedroom windy and see auld Mrs Pedin hanging out her
sheets. But naw, it's like frae amongst the box hedges, the back
green brambles, sprouted a fuckin flaming bastard, tall as a
multi. A red nailed Nick, brazen as fuckit, wi its fingers under
the guttering, jemmying the house tops off. Tar spit – rip o

bullets . . . Then the percussion hits uz like a warm wind. The
wind keeps coming in waves an I'm thinking o Klintnick an
his factories. 'Fuck . . . you . . . Mister! A wish it was you The
Malky battered the other night. I wish it was you he had on the
pub floor, sitting on top of, pounding yer face wi his raw
knuckles. Punch after punch after punch. No rapid, taking his
time tae hit the right fuckin spot. Punters pretending they're no
there, but aw naw, they canny take their eyes off The Malky!
Bob Blunt wi his frozen pint. A wish it was you he stood over,
Mister President, unzipped himself an pished on. Yer torn gub
full o pish! 'Feed the Bear!' That's what I'd be shoutin' 'Feed
the Bear!' As he hammered yer fuckin melon. The sod brother
leaps . . . He's off! Leaps intae fresh air . . . leaps right off the
wreck an is rolling doon the side o the dump, bouncing off bits
o metal. He struggles tae free himself frae this barbed wire,
leaves his torn jacket behind. He's screaming something . . . he
shrieks ma wee sister's name.

A nearly catch up wi him doon by Tongo's corner but a rocket
splits a house in two. All around me Dobermans are barking at
the heli-ships. Tongo's standing on his sofa taking pot shots at
them as they skim over. Their shadows like fuckin thunder
clouds. It's raining bricks. A pick ma way gingerly through the
slavvering dogs an am ready tae sprint when a stops in ma
tracks. Along the street, level wi the top deck o the tenements,
floats this Blackcat heli-ship. It's fuckin huge, know? The
downdraft frae its rotor blades sweeps rubbish before it.
Bonkers, but inside all the racket a can hear the sound of
empty beer cans clankin along the gutter. Wan o the pilots
spots me. Locks onto ma thermal image. A see the cannon
swivel round, am about to gee masel the God's Bless, know,
but then his partner slaps him on the shoulder and points to
Tongo directly below them. Two pilots look at each other . . .

You can tell behind their visors they've finally got the gag –
they've started laughing. The canon changes direction and
punches holes in Tongo's house like the breeze blocks made o
talc powder. The hedge goes. I can see bits o sofa erupting into
the air. His Dobermans are flayed by huge chains. A canny
believe it but when the stour gets a window blown in it . . .
there's Tongo at the corner o the building, sniping frae behind

a rose bush, spitting ball bearings into the breach o his air gun an letting rip . . . Then his heed turned intae a poppy. Splat! A poppy that is too big for his torso an after a few nanos he sort of totters out o sight. Heed turned into a poppy, never seen that before, know?

*Gunk.*

I pull back the concrete slab covering the bomb shelter in our back green. Maggie's got her curlers in, flicking through a fanzine, and NAW, she huzny seen Cockroach. She doesny want to see that creep.

A run upstairs but the house is empty. The windies are blown in. The living room door is off its hinges. A tack the double-page spread back onto the wall an sort o awkwardly, stupidly, salute the photo o Commander X, the leader o the terrorists. The Gaffer. Everyone knows her cryptic slogan: 'It's no freedom but Resistance – none shall survive!'

A crash oot on the sofa. The sod brother's toast, must be? That's what I'm thinking. I kick ma trainers off – there's gunk stuck to the bottom of them. Burger gunk. Gunk frae a burger machine. That's Tongo . . . his Dobermans . . . Cockroach.

*The telly comes back into life.*

NEWS. 'The US and European Fed (*Static.*) reinstate all transmissions in accordance with (*Static.*) Protocol 22 (*Static.*) Collateral disruption shall not impede reciprocal (*Static*) the freedom of information. (*Static.*) The universal – self evident. (*Static.*) This is not a clash of civilisations. Information cannot be denied our citizens . . . ' (*Static. Transmission ends.*)

*Brazil.*

DODDY. Suddenly the super screen flickers intae life . . . There's this wee dot, know, this wee dot. An this wee dot swells intae this tiny revolving orb – it's the earth, know? The orb grows and grows intae this marble bowling baw. It's turning in the vastness o space.

The camera rockets towards the planet. Thrill, know, to make oot the continents. The shot zooms until you see rivers like fat arteries feeding the lung o South America. You can make oot

islands off along the coasts. It's wan o they nature programmes.
A love nature programmes. It's ma favourite TV. Then am in
cloud and it's like the smokes surrounding . . . a volcano . . .
A love volcanoes. The smoke blows away and it's Brazil. Must
be.

Am o'er the sea. Am o'er the sea cos am flying man. A can
feel on ma face the spray from they waves turnin in the grey
ocean. There's the jaggy scar o land ahead. Waves scudding
ashore. Then it's sugar loaf. Loads of loafs. Somethin's
missing. A clock scree frae a giant building crashed face first
doon the side o a mountain. Must be Jesus kissin the slums,
know – what a snogger he is. A turn inland no wanting to look
at the city    I can smell the burning malls. I can sense ma wee
sister stonnin in the doorway staring at us. A can hear her
calling ma name. It doesny matter . . . doesny matter what
name you use hen, know? This time am no coming back. I
look doon. A hiv tae. At first all the trees are burnt matchsticks
an there's millions o people, moving, crawling in huge swarms.
Then, crossing this border am above forests. An a can see ma
shadow dipping into green troughs . . . am sitting in ma Dad's
chair. I feel tears rolling doon ma jug. I think o the earth . . .
the earth an that, know? A don't mind becoming the worst
fucker they can imagine! An I'm on ma feet and I fuckin
plunge run right intae the telly . . .

Branches lash ma face as a crash through. I can smell smoke
an somewhere an alarm's ringing. I plough intae a bank of
knotted roots. Bounce intae this broon river. Bubbles stream
up frae the air trapped in ma clothes an . . . mud jams intae
ma mouth . . . stanes . . . silt. Everythin's slow . . . as a curls up
. . . intae this baw. An at last . . . at last . . . it's beautiful.

But it doesny last.

Ma Da wants his chair back. 'That's ma seat, you know a
canny sit fuckin anywhere else. Selfish wee bastard.' A don't
think am even sitting in his fuckin chair. A can hear ma Ma
shuffling in her blue slippers. 'Geez the God's Bless, son. A
need it. A don't know what road to go doon. A need it NOW!'
Maggie's shaking me. Why does Maggie want to marry
someone called Gentle-whistle when she grows up? A ken I'm

no hearing words right. Da's shouting about ma filter. 'Ez
filter's fuckin bust. That's the trouble wi him, his filter doesny
work right. Look at him, words piping out him, like a burst
cludgy. Get this cunt seen tae! Look wit he's done to the fuckin
box! Too much fresh stretch between him an everything else.
That's an evil wee scunner.' The old boy's prodding me wi his
foot. Setting himself up for a good kick. That's his style.
There's something between us, me an ma old man, see, that
isny there. Ma Maw pushes him oot the way. Her spittle is
sprayed onto ma face. She must be bent over me. I can taste
the cake she was gobblin earlier, afore the raid. The greasy
cream. Then someone, someone else is wiping my face clean.
No one of ma mob – it's too soft. Nae soft like that round here.
I can feel someone gee'n uz the God's Bless. Must be myself.
Sometimes a do that. Gee masel the sign o the Dirty Beast.
Then Maggie's putting me to bed the way she puts ma Da tae
bed when he's blind drunk in his yellow long johns. She's
tucking me into ma kip. Nae agro. 'Is this the day?' Am sayin
tae her. 'Is this the day?' 'Naw, naw,' she's sayin, 'you're not
alone, Doddy. It canny be the day, cos you're not alone . . .
You're no alone. Shhhh.'

*Scrap Motors.*

A open ma eyes. Am up in the dump. Stonnin on a rust bucket.
Just stonning on top of a stack o scrap motors, spout mouthing
it. Not loud or nothing. No nuts or anything. No heard by
anybody. Which is how a love to talk it. On ma tod. Discussing
the privy . . . stuff. No thoughts, more than that . . . signs sort
of. No minding what comes out. Just like the God's Bless. Not
that a can hear the words I'm saying. I'm more and more deaf
to them.

I look round. I don't get it. Somehow I'm doon wandering
about, looking for that angel. Maybe I'm dreamin it – maybe
I'm in detention wearing the old punishment hood. Floating
in and oot o consciousness. But that's no it, cos everything
looks . . . feels so clear. Washed in tinkle. It's no right to be
this clear. A must have ran oot the hoose. Ran through the
scheme. The tag on my ankle is going ballistic. There should
be pain but I canny feel any.

I canny find that plaster angel anywhere. There's a burnt hole where she used to be. Took off like a shooting star in reverse gear. She's got the fuck oot o here, know? A can see it's the right spot cos a can see Cockroach's jacket flapping on the barbed wire. The arms o his jacket, like that, reaching out for somethin, know? A can see the whole scheme frae here. There's The Goody Two-Shoes an the rust on the roofs. Sort of red. Burnt orange. Now's it's turnt Nomadic Glow, that's number 21. Purple bing . . . that's number 57. Orinoco broon . . . Banana Dream . . . Lusty Lavender – her favourite. Now it's turnt 97. 97. Ma wee sister reading them out. Me holding the torch

*Long pause.*

A'm no lookin for anything that lasts. Um a?

I used to think. A used to think . . . There's somethin unforgiven, know? There's something unforgiven. The way one thing becomes the other. The way wan thing becomes the other.

*End.*

## Glossary

*a, a've, am* – I, I've, I'm

*bam* – idiot

*baws* – balls

*breenge* – to move impetuously

*clockin* – watching

*deeks* – looks

*didny* – did not

*dirty beast* – priest

*doesny* – does not

*dool* – sorrow (doleful)

*doolie-doomster* – a spectre

*doon* – down

*evermair* – evermore

*ey* – always

*frae* – from

*fur* – for

*gauzy* – frail, flimsy

*geez, ge'z, ge'uz* – give us

*glaikit* – senseless, silly, thoughtless

*gonny* – going to

*gowden* – golden

*gub* – mouth

*hae, hiv* – have

*hamshankers* – wankers

*his* – has

*hunders* – hundreds

*intae* – into

*loupin* – throbbing, as of a bruise

*Ma, Maw* – mother

*ma* – my

*mair* – more

*masel* – myself

*May-gobs* – May rainshowers

*melt*   head

*nae* – no

*noo* – now

*numptees* – fools

*o* – of

*oot* – out

*Smeagolly* – in an ingratiating, sycophantic manner (like Smeagol/Gollum in *Lord of the Rings*)

*stane* – stone (*stane-loupin* – bruised by stone)

*stoating* – bouncing

*stonning* – standing

*stour* – dust in motion, chaff, flour, any powdered substance

*tae* – to

*Tagues* – Catholics

*tain* – taken

*a tolly* – a turd

*toon* – town

*ur* – are (*ur yi* – are you)

*uz* – us

*wance* – once

*windies* – windows

*wiz* – was

*wizny* – was not

*yer* – your

*yi* – you

*yous* – second-person personal pronoun